I0149089

Anyone's Daughter

Amanda Todd, Bullying, Anonymous and the Dark Side of the Internet

Anyone's Daughter: Amanda Todd, Bullying, Anonymous and the Dark Side of the Internet
by Quinn Alexander

Published by The Meager Press of Toronto, themeagerpress.com
©2016 The Meager Press

Cover image by Wikimedia Commons

ISBN: 978-0-9939950-4-0

Anyone's Daughter

Amanda Todd, Bullying, Anonymous and the Dark Side of the Internet

By Quinn Alexander

To all the bullied

Introduction

By Jerry Langton

A few years ago, I pitched the idea of a book about the Amanda Todd tragedy to my regular publisher. At the time, I believed it was an important story, but I also thought that the narrative that most people were being given and accepting was misguided and overly managed. To me at least, it appeared that most people were ignoring a serious problem — men abusing and extorting young people over the internet with what seemed like impunity — while concentrating on how best to show their disapproval for bullying in school.

My publisher turned it down, saying that it was too sad a story and that nobody would want to read about it. I disagreed.

So I shopped it around. It did not take long for me to find a smaller publisher who was interested. The advance they offered me was about one-tenth of what I was used to, but I thought the story was important and not being reported accurately, so I started to talk with them.

While that was happening, Nova Scotia's Rehtaeh Parsons took her own life in circumstances that had many parallels with Todd's situation. To me, it seemed natural to include her story in the book, and to change the focus toward the dangers facing Canadian girls that other people otherwise might not be aware of.

But I had doubts as to whether I was actually the right person to write the book. I wasn't sure if I was sensitive enough. So when the publisher told me that they'd like me to include an American example of a girl being driven to suicide over sexual interference "so it doesn't seem so much like a Canadian thing," I moved on.

Years later, when I found out that Quinn was approaching the subject, I was more than happy to hand over my notes and sources.

The result in Anyone's Daughter, which I think sheds light on the more serious crimes that were committed against Todd. It's not the book I would have written, but that's probably a good thing.

Chapter 1: The Video We All Saw

Y ou've seen the video. If you hadn't, you almost certainly wouldn't know the name Amanda Todd, and you definitely wouldn't be reading this book. But like tens of millions of other people, you did see her video, and couldn't help but be moved by it.

It's chilling, in part because you know the girl is dead by the time you've seen it. Of course, the video was posted to YouTube while Amanda was still alive, but almost nobody saw it before she died.

The video itself is clever and well done, and at the same time heart wrenching. In black and white, an obviously young girl holds up pieces of paper with hand-written notes on them and drops them, urging the viewer to read and wait for the next one. The first one simply contains the word "hello!" with a little heart at the bottom of the exclamation point — as if to remind the viewer of her vulnerability and youth.

Dropping cards like she does is an excellent attention-grabbing technique, pioneered in 1965 by director D.A. Pennebaker for the Bob Dylan song Subterranean Homesick Blues. Although Amanda Todd loved pop music, it's unlikely she had ever seen the clip. After all, it was made more than thirty years before she was born. She might not even have known who Bob Dylan was.

Instead, she probably got the idea from a very similar video produced a few months earlier by a popular young American YouTube user named MollyDoyle18. The video Molly posted described her own struggles with depression and loneliness; and police have determined that the Amanda and Molly communicated in private online, although it's not likely they ever met in person.

The reason you've heard of Amanda Todd and not Molly Doyle is because Todd committed suicide shortly after posting her video to YouTube. Doyle is alive and, according to what she's posted online recently, feeling better and aspiring to become a novelist. In fact, after Amanda's suicide, Molly commented on her video: "Rest in peace and fly high to Amanda Todd. I was just messaging her about almost a week ago, and I just found out that she has taken her life... Bullying is NEVER okay. Rest easy, Amanda. I'm so sorry to her family."

Lots of people post personal videos online and lots of people commit suicide, but few of either become household names like Amanda Todd did. Though it's true that some people checked her video out due to their own morbid curiosity, that would not explain the tens of millions of views, nor the tsunami of media coverage it received. In fact, a video that showed the shocked and dismayed reactions of other teens watching Amanda's video has more than 31 million views of its own. The difference with Amanda seems to be that her video struck a chord with people after her death. Here we see a young girl, someone who should be happy and full of life, terrorized into a situation in which suicide seemed to be the only answer.

In the video, she tells the story of how she was a ninth grader — that means she was just 14 years old — and that she enjoyed chatting with friends online. She was encouraged, she writes, to lift her top on camera. She did.

It was a bad idea. Someone — she had no idea who, just a guy with the fictitious name Tyler Boo — later told her he'd show the picture of her to her friends and family unless she performed three nude online "shows" for him.

Amanda was defiant. But he wasn't bluffing.

Soon, almost everyone she knew was given a link to her flashing picture. She was taunted at school and visited in the middle of the night by police. She thought they'd help her. After all, she had proof she was being blackmailed. They only told her to stay off the internet.

Her peer group became relentless in their bullying, taunting her in person and online. She began to show signs of depression. She started drinking and taking drugs. She started self-mutilating. The stress became so bad she had to change schools.

But the person who was extorting her found her new school and repeated the process, showing her new friends and classmates the picture of her flashing when she was just 14. The kids at her new high school were no kinder than her first. Those who didn't outright bully her ignored her.

Desperately lonely, she slept with a boy she had known — the only person, she said, that was still talking to her — even though she knew he had a girlfriend.

Angered, the girlfriend and her allies beat Amanda up.

Distraught, Amanda attempted suicide by drinking bleach.

That only intensified the bullying. The kids at her school urged her to kill herself. She tried again, this time with the antidepressant pills she was taking. Again, she was rescued.

Then she made the video, desperate for someone to come to her aid. In her own words, "I'm stuck... whats left of me now... nothing stops. I have nobody... I need someone :(My name is Amanda Todd."

Nobody did. In fact, the first comments on the video (long since removed) were abusive.

On October 10, 2012 — just weeks before what would have been her 16th birthday — Amanda took her own life.

***

The story, of course, did not end there. Amanda's video went viral. It was soon discovered by social and then mainstream media, and it became a world-wide phenomenon.

The story of a girl, lured into flashing by an unknown predator on the internet, then bullied essentially to her death was an irresistible story. It raised questions about sexual predation, bullying, sexism, internet security and global law enforcement.

The mainstream media carried the day, concentrating on bullying, rather than the more difficult question of who had extorted her. Soon, vigils, rallies and other anti-bullying events were held all over the world in Amanda's name.

But then things got ugly again. People started bullying Amanda again. Thousands of people wrote on YouTube and on Facebook that she deserved to be bullied, even to die, because she had lifted her shirt when she was just 14. Thousands more made what they considered funny memes centered around Amanda drinking bleach or hanging herself.

The backlash was as shocking as the original story. People were openly mocking the death of a child, the victim of a sex crime yet, most of them under the cloak of internet anonymity.

The story of what happened is not primarily about Amanda Todd the individual. She was a little girl who was taken advantage of, made some mistakes in her life and was badgered into suicide. The story would almost certainly have ended there if she had not made her video or it had not been discovered by media.

And, in another era, it probably would have ended soon afterward with people feeling good about themselves and their anti-bullying efforts.

But it didn't. Instead, Amanda's torment, her video and her suicide led us down a path that showed us the ugly side of our culture. How men prey on women and girls (and sometimes boys) on the internet, how some in society believe that the victims are the ones to blame when it comes to sex crimes if they are female and how people can be empowered to say the ugliest and most hurtful things if they believe they won't have to take responsibility for them.

Chapter 2: Everyone has Something to Say

If ever there was a name with magical qualities, it's not Beetlejuice or Voldemort, it's Amanda Todd. Mention the name Amanda Todd on the internet, and everybody seems to have something to say. If you're not already familiar with the avalanche of media related to her, Google her name. But be careful, you might see and read things that are very disturbing — potentially even illegal.

Thousands of people went to social media after her suicide to tell the world what they thought of her, share their opinions on bullying and instruct girls on how they think they should behave. Almost as many took to the same and other venues to laugh at Amanda, to mock her short life and tragic end, to instruct young women about their place in the world. Some even started scams in brazen attempts to make a quick buck off the attention paid to her story.

But when I tried to get people to talk about her for a book, the silence was disturbing. Everyone who had something to say suddenly changed their minds.

I contacted hundreds of people and the overwhelming majority refused to speak on the record, and those that did asked me not to use their real names. Many of the people I spoke with became angry, even vaguely threatening, that I would want them to talk about the events leading up to Amanda Todd's death and implored me to "leave the poor family alone" and to "let the girl rest in peace."

I believed that position to be an odd, even specious, response because I found almost all of them through comments they had made on social media regarding Todd and her death.

They had taken the time to give their two cents about Todd when they felt there would be no follow up, but once they were on record, they had decided it was in bad taste to say anything about the same subject.

Indeed, that's the way it's been with Todd. Millions and millions of people watched her YouTube video — a public suicide note of sorts — and many of them liked, commented on and forwarded any mention of her on social media. Many of the same people later wore ribbons and attended vigils and rallies in her honor.

It became fashionable to care about Todd and girls like her. Anti-bullying campaigns — many of them spurred into existence or at least greater prominence due to the coverage of Amanda's suicide — swelled in their numbers of supporters and contributors. But when it came to actually finding out the truth about how and why she died, people seemed to be a lot less interested. It would appear that they were more prepared to assuage their communal grief (and perhaps guilt) by lighting candles and condemning bullying than actually finding the person who extorted her, tormented her and eventually led her to become so distraught that she believed suicide was the only answer.

While it is true that it was primarily children she knew from the three high schools she attended that tormented Todd without mercy and even assaulted her physically, they had bullied her — like lots of other children — for one reason or another at a level she found tolerable for most of her life. But it was only after her extortionist distributed illegal pictures of her exposed breasts that their bullying became aggressive, personal and physical.

And it should be noted that none of those kids have ever been identified or in any way punished for their individual actions. Dozens of high school students directed hurtful posts at Amanda on Facebook, and several urged her to kill herself, even after she had attempted suicide. Their identities are not well known by the public, but they are among their peers. I've been told that some of them have since claimed online to have been Amanda's friends and have even been involved in anti-bullying events in her name.

The spur that intensified their bullying from occasional name-calling to ritual abuse and prompted her sorrow, alcohol and drug use, self-mutilation and suicide was that a man who she had never met in person blackmailed her.

Without his intervention, Todd in all likelihood would have continued her life — described by everyone I have spoken with as not exactly idyllic, but certainly tolerable — much as she had before his extortion attempt. It could be argued that he, in effect, was ultimately responsible for her death.

But finding him seemed secondary to the people in mainstream media and government. Instead, the concentrated their efforts on raising awareness of bullying. While attempting to reduce bullying in school is a noble undertaking, it seems to distract from the actual cause of Todd's death.

Of course, getting to the bottom of the story isn't going to bring Todd back. But finding out how extortionists who prey on children online can help prevent it from happening to more of them.

***

After her death, a remarkable number of people thought it was appropriate to share their opinions of Amanda Todd with the rest of the world. In the wake of her heart-wrenching video, hundreds of thousands of people took to the internet to make public their opinion on her life, death and her character.

It's just how we do things now.

After combing through the thousands and thousands of YouTube comments and videos and the Facebook comments, I have found that there are four words people frequently use to describe Amanda Todd. Depending on which side they take, people tend call her an angel, a princess, a slut or a whore. Of course, almost none of those people ever met Amanda while she was alive, and fewer still helped her when things got tough. But still they feel free, almost duty-bound, in huge numbers, to judge her in a public forum.

The truth is that she was actually none of those things that people call her. She was just a kid. A kid who made some mistakes, like all kids do.

Away from the internet, few people would talk openly about their opinions on a victim of a sex-related crime — especially a minor like Todd.

Much of the social media commentary — certainly among those who call her slut and whore, just like her school bullies did — focused on the opinion that Todd crossed a line when she bared her chest online. They intimated that she invited, even deserved, her unwanted attention by doing so. But no matter what she did on camera (and there is still great debate as to what she did actually do) that it was recorded and used to extort her is the actual crime.

They should be reminded that she did not, could not, have brought the tragedy that befell her upon herself, nor is it even remotely possible that she could ever have deserved any of what happened to her — it's the same kind of opinion that maintains short skirts are the root cause of rape. In fact, the opinion that Todd deserved to be extorted because somebody had something she didn't want other people to see denies that extortion is even a crime.

Many on social media expressed the opinion that because they believed that Todd transgressed their own personal concept of sexual mores by flashing and then later having sex with another girl's boyfriend, that she deserves public shaming and humiliation.

However, nowhere could I find anyone calling out the boy involved, even though he initiated the tryst with Amanda, admitting to her that he already had a steady girlfriend. Clearly, the lessons from Nathaniel Hawthorne's 1850 masterpiece, The Scarlet Letter, have gone unheeded in many corners of our society.

The idea that anyone could hold those opinions in this day and age is actually quite frightening from a civil liberties perspective. But that didn't stop thousands of people from voicing that opinion in public, though often through the veil of internet anonymity.

These people felt a need to tell the world, Amanda's friends, her parents and even her tormentors exactly what they thought and felt about a girl they knew almost nothing about. With the scantest of evidence, they were ready to canonize or damn a kid, really just a kid, for what she might or might not have done, and what happened to her because of it.

That's why this book isn't as much about Amanda as it is about the sides of our society that her tragic suicide exposed.

But it's important to know something about the girl herself. Much of what I have learned has come from people who say they were her friends or acquaintances, but none were willing to let me use their actual names, and some were still minors. The outrage over what has happened in the wake of her death has made them even more reluctant to identify themselves in case they too are dragged into the ugly debate, the finger-pointing and name-calling that still exists even now.

***

Amanda Michelle Todd was born in November 1996, which would put her squarely in a cultural grouping that some call Generation Y and others call the Millennials. According to the Pew Research Center, Millennials are less likely to identify with or trust institutions and far more likely to put their trust in their network of friends and acquaintances. Similarly, Inc. magazine reported that

Millennials are more prone to acts of passion and spontaneity that generations before them, and are much more likely to take risks.

Her age also meant that she has never existed in a world that was not dominated and enlightened by the Internet.

From all reports, she grew up as a more or less ordinary Canadian girl, although she is said to have had a mild learning disability that led to a barely detectable speech impediment. She sometimes did poorly in school, despite being described as intelligent by people who knew her. She was regularly teased by other children for her low grades, and called "retard" by some. At the time, the bullying she received appeared to fall within societal norms of acceptability, and it did not prevent her from being known as a generally happy and gregarious kid. She was, her mother told The Vancouver Sun, once particularly upset in high school when a teacher read all of the class members' marks on a quiz aloud and Amanda's was a failing grade, the lowest in the class.

According to many sources, Amanda was a very busy girl. She was involved in competitive swimming, gymnastics, soccer and ice hockey. Her favorite athletic activity, as I have been told repeatedly, was cheerleading, which she did for almost half of her short life. She was a member of the G Force Gym Vancouver All Stars, a Port Coquitlam-based cheerleading team, for six years. The showmanship of cheerleading neatly dovetailed with Amanda's love of singing and dancing. Several people who claim to know her have told me that she wanted to grow up to be a pop singer, and surviving evidence supports that theory.

Her parents separated when she was in seventh grade, and she went to live with her father, small business owner Norm Todd. Two years later, she moved in with her mother, assistive technology teacher Carol Todd.

While it is not common for a father to be given custody, especially of a girl, none of the credible sources I have spoken to believe that Amanda placement with her father was made for any reason other than convenience. She moved from his Maple Ridge home to her mother's Port Coquitlam house only after she had been relentlessly bullied out of two different Maple Ridge high schools.

From a very early age, Amanda was well acquainted with social media.

It has been widely published that she had her own YouTube channel called SomebodytoKnow, on which she sang covers of contemporary pop songs. At the time, it was a commonplace habit with kids her age. It was well known among them that Justin Bieber — and Todd was by all accounts a huge fan of the Canadian pop sensation — started his career by singing on YouTube.

In fact, Todd appears to have made social media something of a hobby, and seems to have started at a young age. Most social-media sites have age restrictions that would have made Todd ineligible, but it's commonplace for kids to fudge their ages online. After all, they know that nobody's checking.

Online research by several sources concludes that Todd had accounts on several social media sites, including Facebook, MySpace and others. She was also member of at least four video-streaming sites by the end of 2010, when she was 14. They included TinyChat, Hi5, Stickam and BlogTV.

The big difference between these sites and the better-known video sites like YouTube and Vimeo is that they allow the user to broadcast live rather than just recorded video. That means that users can communicate with other users in real time, like a video chat, but with an audience.

That makes the sites popular with many teens who enjoy talking with friends — and also to strangers. The anonymity of the internet (or at least the belief of anonymity) allows users to present themselves in ways they would not ordinarily because they believe they have the ability to abandon their real-life persona or audience if things don't work out the way they want them to.

According to a study on adolescent online behavior by Azy Barak and Meyran Boniel-Nissim at Israel's Haifa University:

"The sense of anonymity and invisibility experienced by Internet users promotes their confidence to express thoughts and feelings. Furthermore, users do not feel committed to the offline social codes — including attire, nonverbal gestures, and eye contact — when interacting online with other people."

On those sites, Todd had many accounts with varying degrees of anonymity, and went by a number of assumed names, including AnnouncingAmanda, isabella100555, xXAmandaXx and, most frequently, cutiielover — with its distinctive spelling.

Virtually all of what she posted in her lifetime has since been deleted.

A YouTube account in her mother's name maintains a collection of Amanda's singing videos and carefully monitors the comments on them.

The earliest still-existing evidence of Todd available online is, not surprisingly, a video on YouTube. It's called Amanda Todd MSN Conversation (Must See). It was posted in April 2009, when Todd would have been 12, but the poster describes it as "really old." The video shows a conversation between a young girl (who if she is not Amanda, bears a remarkable resemblance to her), maybe 11, and a boy maybe a couple of years older. Her handle is Cutiie <3 (note the double "i" in cutiie) and his is Tomas – Married to the greatest Girl EVER! Their conversation, caught in progress, is as follows:

Tomas – Married to the greatest Girl EVER!: y a in front of 376 people too (he begins to start chewing on a shoelace)

Cutiie <3: why are u covering your fucken face

Tomas – Married to the greatest Girl EVER!: idk (slang for I don't know)

Cutiie <3: the thing I like about u is ur smile, laugh and how u laugh at everything (pause as he smiles, revealing the shoelace in his mouth) wtf ? keep it comin... keep goin eww lmao

At this point, their conversation is interrupted as the boy gets a chat from another girl, calling herself Lisa.

Tomas – Married to the greatest Girl EVER!: ily (slang for I love you)

Lisa: ily tooooooooooooo :P soooooo ? what do you want to talk about ???????

The boy then goes back to chatting with Cutiie <3. The kids then send each other "nudges" (online acknowledgements like Facebook pokes) and laugh.

Tomas – Married to the greatest Girl EVER!: psh don't nudge me ("psh" is a dismissive interjection, like "whatever")

Cutiie <3: qhT what?

Tomas – Married to the greatest Girl EVER!: qht? Wtf lmao (she laughs)

Cutiie <3: omg

Tomas – Married to the greatest Girl EVER!: omg omg omfg

Cutiie <3: ur a loser !! (they laugh)

Tomas – Married to the greatest Girl EVER!: qht

Cutiie <3: omfg stop making fun of me ☹g

The chat then ends.

While it's not the most interesting or enlightening transcript in history, its existence does indicate that Todd (if it is indeed her, and I'm absolutely certain that it is), was conversant with video streaming and live chat at a very early age.

It also shows that her name meant something to some people in the YouTube community; certainly enough that a simple chat with her was recorded, stored and then rebroadcast later. The fact that the video gives her full name in the title and is labelled a "must see" in 2009 — long before she became known to mainstream media in 2012 — indicates that she was already well known online, at least by her own group.

And there is one comment, since deleted, on the video that's more than a little disturbing. Someone calling himself Coot19 wrote: "wait till she's a little older m8 she can flash her mosquito's then." That has been interpreted in social media as a reference to her showing her breasts.

That comment received a direct reply from an account called Peter Quill that read:

"LLLLLLLLLLLLLLLLLLLOOOOOOOOOOOOOOOOOOOOOOOOOO
OOOOOOOOOOOOOOOOOOOOOOOOOOOOOOOOOOOOOOOOOOO
OOOOOOOOOOOOOOOOOOOOOOOOOOOOOOOOOOOOOOOOOOO
OOOOOOOOOOOOOOOOOOOOOOOLLLLLLLLLLLLLLLLLLLLL
LLLLLLLLLLLLLLLLLLLLLLLLLLLLLLLLLLLLLLLLLLLL
LLLLLLLLLLLLL She already did that."

Both comments were posted after Todd's death, and the owners of the Coot19 and Peter Quill accounts did not answer requests to talk to me.

Interestingly, MSN chat back then displayed the email address of who you were chatting with. Cutiie <3's address was "mandy_kinz11@hotmail.com." That same address shows up one other time on the internet.

One October 5, 2006, an Indianapolis-based band that described itself as "pop country" called BackTraked put an ad on Topix.com's Indiana University Indianapolis NCAA basketball fan page looking for a lead singer.

Most of the 56 answers were from Midwest-based singers looking for a tryout, but one — posted April 2, 2008, when Todd was 11 — was from mandy_kinz11@hotmail.com, who introduced herself as Amanda from Vancouver. It read:

Hey, Um.... I was just wondering if I could be in your band. I love to sing and I have been singing since I was 2 years old. I love concerts and I am not afraid to dance and move around in front of a big crowd. If you want to get to know me more just email me or add me to your msn at mandy_kinz11@hotmail.com I hope you think I'm cool! Bye Bye!

BackTraked no longer exists as a band.

Also in 2009, someone calling themselves SiKstep9 posted a video of a junior high school-aged boy, probably the poster himself, dancing. Although the comment from isabella100555 has been deleted, SiKstep9 responded to it by writing: "lmfao, who is this?" Not long after, someone named reanimationb0mb2 added: "isabella is amanda todd she's a real bitch." When I reached out to him, he did not reply.

Amanda joined another video streaming site, UStream, on November 22, 2010, just after her 14th birthday. She used her real name, said she was from Vancouver, and described herself by writing: "I sinnnnng, and love to hang out ! ;]" She also had other UStream accounts called Amanda Showw ☺, AnnouncingAmanda, Announcing Amanda, JUSTIN BIEBER OMMG, JUSTIN BIEBER OMMMG and Mandaa&Shyy, with her friend Shylah Watson. Two videos still exist on the Mandaa&Shyy account, which has the tagline "we are amazing." They are uneventful, featuring grainy, barely audible images of what appears to be Amanda hanging out with her friend Shylah and listening to music. About nine minutes into the video, Todd points out that a moderator is watching them, and Watson replies that "it's because they like me."

None of that seems particularly worrisome. Yes, Todd (if it was her) did drop a misspelled F-bomb on the MSN chat video when she was 11 or so, but most kids that age like to swear around their friends when their parents aren't around. She just seems like a little girl having fun and trying to further her pursuit of a future career as a pop singer.

Chapter 3: A Lapse in Judgment

B
ut then she flashed. If you think you know what happened when Todd lifted her shirt for her webcam, you're almost certainly wrong. That's because it has often been reported, or at least intimated, in both the mainstream and social media, that she was chatting with a single person, an older man, an adult certainly, who persuaded her to flash.

It's just not true. At least it isn't accurate when it comes to the picture of her that was widely distributed. It's a fallacy built up by a lack of understanding of how youth culture and internet culture actually work. And it's also a scenario that's more palatable to those who want to believe that Todd was acting against her will or, at least, her better judgment.

Here's how it the misconception happened: People in the media (a generation at least once removed from Todd and her peer group) grew up with the concept of electronic communication as a one-on-one process, like a telephone call, and assumed it happened that way in this case. They took what little they actually knew about the event — remember that nobody who knew anything about the event, and that includes law enforcement, wanted to talk about it at the time — and shaped it to fit a niche they could comprehend. And it makes a better story because it makes sense to most people that an older man would prey upon an innocent young girl in such a way.

But the event itself didn't happen that way, and it ignores a much more sinister truth.

Along with traditional one-on-one communications, many young people have grown adept at a more modern approach to communication — self-broadcasting. Just as you might wish all of your friends a Happy Thanksgiving at once with a post on Facebook, kids of Todd's age group are just as likely to broadcast their thoughts and actions over video-streaming sites to hundreds, even thousands, of people, many of them strangers.

Here's how it works. Laptops, tablets and handheld devices are equipped with increasingly high-resolution cameras that can shoot and record video. When someone using that device accesses one of the many video-streaming sites, he or she can either watch live video streams or broadcast their own. With some video-streaming sites, like Chatroulette, your video is matched with another random user. With others, like BlogTV, your video can be viewed by friends you approve, and still others allow any user to watch your show.

Many teens get an inflated sense of pride from large audiences and can compete aggressively for viewers. And that's where the problems start. Competition for viewers can lead some teens to go to what we might consider extreme lengths to attract them. That can include nudity and even on-cam masturbation — often at the request of their audience.

The New York Times published an article in 2005 about a 13-year-old boy whose first forays on his webcam were met with dozens of unsolicited requests for nudity. Some offered him money, and one even helped him set up a PayPal account. Before long, he was charging $50 for a three-minute session of shirtless conversation. "I figured, I took off my shirt at the pool for nothing," he told them. "So, I was kind of like, what's the difference?" But his shows later evolved to the point at which he was masturbating on camera daily for as many as 1,500 paying customers.

Webcam nudity has become so prevalent in the consciousness of users of video sites that girls and some boys who use them find themselves inundated with entreaties to take their clothes off and more, and can find their inboxes full of graphic photos.

Because of that, and other reasons, teens rarely use their real names on video-streaming sites, relying on that thread of semi-anonymity to keep their parents and other potentially concerned parties away from their accounts.

Some adults are aware of what sometimes happens on these sites, and take advantage of it. Generally referred to as "lurkers" or "creepers," there are people (often adults) who watch videos on teen-oriented streaming sites in hopes of catching some nudity. Sometimes they might pose as fellow teens, but most of them — from what I have been told — just stay quiet and hope for the best. One girl I spoke with who broadcast on Stickam, but said she "never showed," told me that creepers were a huge problem for her. "I'd be talking about something, and all of a sudden I'd get a message saying 'flash' or 'show us your tits;' then came the dick pics," she said. "It actually made me leave Stickam, it wasn't worth it."

Of course, any image of nudity by anyone under 18 (ages differ in various jurisdictions) can constitute child pornography, which is illegal and can be dealt with very harshly. In fact, such is the hysteria over child pornography in our culture that, in many cases, sentencing for distribution of child pornography can be harsher than sentencing for physical sexual abuse of children.

Several popular self-broadcasting sites — including BlogTV and the now-notorious Stickam — have been shut down, in a large part because of underage nudity and sexual content, although BlogTV is making a comeback. In 2009 alone, three Stickam users were arrested for sexual assault or sexual interference for what they presented on the site or what they persuaded others to do.

The video-streaming sites can potentially be held responsible for any illegal images that they host, so they work to prevent it from happening by employing moderators — people who watch suspicious broadcasts and shut them down if they see anything potentially illegal. Of course, it's not economically feasible for sites to moderate every broadcast, so they tend only to watch broadcasts with unusually high numbers of viewers, especially those by repeat offenders.

Amanda joined BlogTV on November 26, 2010, the day before her 14th birthday. According to several sources I have spoken with who would rather not be named and several journalists who have spoken with the same or similar sources, not long after she joined, Amanda was on Chatzppl, a BlogTV video-streaming channel specifically designed for 13- to 15-year-olds. Under heavy encouragement from a number of viewers — and despite warnings that moderators could be looking in — Amanda pulled up her top and flashed her breasts for 191 viewers. At least one of them captured the moment, and saved it as a still photo.

***

Not long after, Todd seems to have come to regret her decision, coming to that point of view either on her own or because of discipline from BlogTV moderators (which I have been told both by sources in pro- and anti-Amanda camps was handed down quickly and in no uncertain terms). There is the transcript on the internet of a BlogTV chat dated December 12, 2010 in which cutiielover refers to herself as a "slut" and explains that she's "no longer like that" because "my friends found my pic."

I can't vouch for the transcript's authenticity, but I do know that all of Todd's accounts were terminated by BlogTV on December 17, 2010. And I have been told by several people close to the situation that the incident in question is not the only time Todd flashed on camera. In fact, several sources have told me and it has been attested on several well-regarded online magazines that no fewer than five distinct photos and one video have emerged of Todd flashing. In fact, heavily edited images of what is purported to be

Amanda flashing are still circulating around the easily accessed parts of the internet.

In fact, trading photos of Todd (and others) flashing appears to have been a popular hobby in some circles.

Cooper Fleishman, a respected investigative journalist, found a transcript of a conversation dated December 17, 2010 on a site called 4DS.com (which has since changed owners) in which an account under the name Guest58425 asks for an image of Cutiielover flashing. Another user, perso365, replies "lol, I got enough to be happy."

After some argument as to whether the pictures exist or not, perso365 backs up his claim by posting a link to a photo-storage site, and writes: "I'm in a generous mood, here's a freebie."

Five minutes later, a user named johnnycage posts: "nice flash from cutiielover." Others comment. One says he missed the flash, and another says how much he enjoyed it. Others chime in. One account called aaa asked if Cutiielover actually flashed, and is immediately offered another link to a different storage site by Guest58425.

Another account, Guest57488, then linked to Amanda's AnnouncingAmanda account on BlogTV, essentially identifying Cutiielover as Amanda Todd. He then links to another storage site, writing: "Her tits here lol," and links to her YouTube account as isabella100555, again identifying her.

The conversation then starts to fray, and some guys who sound like regulars start talking about "heroes" and "traitors."

Throughout the conversation, other girls are mentioned in various states of undress, but the excitement is centered around Cutiielover, who appears to be well known among the members of the group. Keep in mind that this conversation was recorded just weeks after Amanda's 14th birthday.

Several of those in the conversation talk about "caps." I would later learn that the term cap is short for screen capture, what the members of this community call photographic or video recordings of online nudity. In their world, people who make or trade caps are called cappers, nudity is called win and those who find win and cap it are referred to as heroes. Traitors are people who try to report caps to the authorities or otherwise make things difficult for heroes.

It's very unlikely that Todd knew anything about any of the excitement she had caused on the internet. Remember, she was just a kid. When she flashed (no matter how many times), she almost certainly thought it was an ephemeral act, one that happened in the moment and that she'd never have to deal with again. She was given a false sense of security, no doubt, by the anonymity offered by her pseudonym and probably had no idea that the software to record her even existed, let alone that there was a community dedicated to collecting and sharing such images.

But there was and is. And they are not kind people.

Not long after the BlogTV flashing incident, Amanda received a message that set out a deal that most people would describe as extortion. It instructed her to do more on-screen nudity, or the capper would share the image he already had with her friends and family.

Amanda refused; probably in youthful hopes that, if she ignored it, the problem would go away on its own.

It didn't. I have been told that the person who sent Amanda the threatening message then set up a Facebook profile posing as a 15-year-old whose parents were planning to move him to Amanda's school after the Christmas break. He used the name Tyler Boo. At the time, "boo" was slang for boyfriend, and many teens were using fictitious last names on Facebook to avoid unwanted attention. Boo, using a profile picture of a nice-looking teenage boy taken from a Google image search, then sent friend requests to all of Amanda's Facebook friends — including classmates and family members — under the guise that he wanted to know some people at the school when he arrived.

Many of them, including Amanda, accepted his friend request. In a few days, Boo was Facebook friends with most of Amanda's classmates and friends. They might have been moved by his story, his appealing photo or they might just have accepted the request without examining it. The number of Facebook friends one had was considered by many teens back then to be a gauge of status — certainly back then, when Facebook was much more popular among teens than it is today — and people of that age group often competed for larger numbers of friends.

After acquiring a large number of Facebook friends in common with Amanda, Boo then allegedly posted a link to the screen capture of her flashing, which he had posted to a popular porn site.

People frequently ask how that sort of thing is possible: How could a picture of an obviously underage girl show up on an immensely popular porn site just like that? It's because porn sites — many of them, at least — don't work like most people think they do.

Although the traditional magazine-style porn sites in which an operator or staff create and/or purchase content and then post it online as a business do exist, they are now in the distinct minority. While there are some sites that pay models to pose or act and a photographer or videographer to record it, other site owners have found that they can get money by taking those and other photos and posting them on their sites. Although outright stealing of content is technically illegal (but rarely prosecuted), many of these sites exist by using the photos and videos the few remaining content-generating sites use to promote their paid material. By accumulating them, even very old ones, they can amass a huge database of images and videos, none of which they had to pay for. They then post the images or videos and make money through advertising, including links to the very sites they took content from.

Even more cost effective are the sites that post user-generated content. Instead of paying for or stealing content, these sites merely set up a place for their users to post it. The reasoning behind these sites is that they are providing a service for people who consider online porn a hobby and want to share free-for-use promotional images and/or self-generated images of willing wives or girlfriends with one another. Again, the revenue comes from advertising.

But just as video-streaming sites say they can't moderate every video made by its members, porn-sharing sites say they can't moderate the often overwhelming number of posts they receive. And most of them can't afford, or say they can't afford, to employ moderators. So they get around the legal responsibility of hosting copyrighted or illegal images by incorporating a button with a message like "report this image" with every entry. That way, any user who sees what they think is an image that violates the rules of the site or laws of their jurisdiction can report it to the site's owner or staff so that it can be removed, reported to authorities and the user who posted it potentially banned from the site or criminally investigated.

I hope that the flaw in that process is obvious. It's like having mice guard cheese. While sites like YouTube, which have a huge audience with a wide variety of interests and moralities, can use user-reporting as a mostly effective way to filter out videos that violate public standards and laws, the concept doesn't work quite as well with porn sites. Because they rely on self-reporting of violations and the users are porn fans, porn-sharing sites can host all manner of material, with its legality at best a gray area. And the owners of the sites have come to realize that they are essentially safe from prosecution if they take down any flagged images.

Amanda's picture was loaded on such a site. Boo then allegedly sent a link to the picture to all of Amanda's Facebook friends with a click-bait style headline — something along the lines of "You Must See This!" (my sources differ on or can't remember exactly what it was).

It was not obvious that the link led to a porn site because the poster used a link-shortener to change its name. Link-shorteners are services (like Google's goo.gl) that take long links and shorten them for use on such character-count limited sites as Twitter. The shortened version usually looks like a jumble of letters and numbers and gives no indication of the name or nature of the site linked to.

Many who received the link — including Amanda — did not click on it, but many others did. One 14-year-old girl who did follow the link identified the photo as Amanda and immediately told her own parents.

The girl knew Amanda from school, but not well. Her parents did not know Amanda's parents, so they called the police, told them what they had seen and provided Amanda's first and last name.

While many communities in the metropolitan Vancouver area have their own police forces, Maple Ridge — where Amanda lived with her father at the time — is served by an RCMP detachment. Some small-town Canadians believe that RCMP officers — who can be from anywhere in Canada and often don't have roots in the communities they serve — are not quite as dedicated to certain situations as local police forces that generally draw their officers from the surrounding area.

They took the issue seriously, but armed with little information apart from the victim's name and school, had a hard time finding her. Finally, at 4 a.m., they knocked on Norm Todd's door. It was, I have been told, quite a scene; as the officers had to knock loud enough to wake the house's occupants. Many have referred to it online later as the cops breaking down the door. They did not.

The RCMP officers then informed Norm and Amanda about what they knew. Norm was appalled, but the CBC later reported that Amanda "played it off as goofing around, and said it wasn't a huge deal."

While Amanda was, in all likelihood, hoping the situation would just go away on its own, it was not going to. Her blackmailer was confident, determined and unafraid of being caught.

The CBC later reported that, on Christmas Eve, Carol Todd received a message on Facebook from an account she did not recognize — it was from what's known by internet cognoscenti as a "throwaway," an email address intended for anonymity, often used one time only. It informed her that Amanda was being blackmailed, and then gave her a brief explanation as to what cappers do, and how Amanda is hardly the only girl to have been extorted by them. Carol, according to the same report, immediately called the RCMP detachment in the town she lived in, Port Coquitlam, and forwarded them the message.

With Christmas break over, Amanda returned to school. Where she lived in Maple Ridge, high school started at eighth grade and ended at twelfth grade, unlike most of Canada and the U.S., where high school begins at ninth or even tenth grade.

Todd attended Westview Secondary. It's a large school by the standards of the area — about 900 students. And, like Maple Ridge itself, its population is mostly white, with some students of East Asian and South Asian descent. It's not regarded as a particularly tough school — although Maple Ridge has a higher-than-average crime rate, particularly for drug offenses and robbery — but it has its assortment of problems.

I was lucky enough to be able to interview someone who knew her there, was in the same grade and some of her classes, under the provision I did not use his real name. So for the purposes of this book, we will call him Michael.

He told me that, before the flashing images surfaced when they were in ninth grade, Todd was neither popular nor truly unpopular. She had some friends, but there were girls — he provided names, but I won't use them — who really didn't like her, and made fun of her "sometimes," often in reference "to her marks and stuff." He said that one of them told him that they found Amanda to be "prissy," and that she made "a big deal" out of showing concern for others, but was also quick to be judgmental. I asked him if he disagreed with that assessment, and he told me that "guys don't talk like that."

He pointed out that students coming to Westview came from a variety of feeder schools and that in the first few months of high school, kids tended to stay with and socialize with their old friends from their old schools. The girls who did not like Todd were generally not from her old school.

Although she tended to keep to her own group, Michael told me that Amanda was friendly and generally easy to get along with, although she "could be sad sometimes."

Others describe her as gregarious and friendly. "I could see that some days were hard for Amanda," said Leah Pells, one of her teachers. "No matter what was happening to her, she cared for all the students in the class, asking other students if they were okay and worrying when they didn't show up for class. She felt things so deeply, which was a blessing and a curse for her."

Michael said that Amanda was acknowledged by the boys in her class as not unattractive, but was not, that he knew of, romantically linked to anyone, although many of the girls were.

Of course, everything changed over the Christmas break. Amanda returned to class January 4, 2011.

While it's unclear how many of the students had seen the actual photo of Amanda or had shared it, knowledge of it, according to Michael's recollection, was widespread. In fact, he said "everybody" knew about it, and most people he knew claimed to have seen it.

He himself had heard of it from a friend he had run into at the ValleyFair mall over Christmas break. The other boy was with his mother and sister, so they had to break free of them to talk. Michael told me that the other boy told him that Amanda was "naked all over the internet" and that he had "seen the pictures," although Michael told me that he doubts those claims in retrospect because the other boy's description of what he'd seen did not mesh with what he had learned later. They are no longer friends.

At first, Michael told me, Todd was greeted with silence and stares. Then giggling. The kids, he said, egged on by the girls who had already decided they did not like Amanda, started calling her "porn star" and "camwhore."

I asked him how she reacted. "She cried and ran out of the class," he said.

Chapter 4: Cappers

As difficult as it might be to picture, the number of people who entice young people to flash or strip, then record it and potentially use those recording for blackmail is actually quite large and surprisingly well organized. In fact, they have (or at least had) an online video awards show posted to YouTube called The Daily Capper. On it, an animated newsreader with a highly distorted voice gives out awards including "cam whore of the year," "capper of the year" and even "best blackmailer." An account known simply as Kody1206 was awarded Blackmailer of the Year for 2010.

But there is dissention and jealousy among the ranks of cappers. On December 23, 2010 — a few hours before the RCMP knocked on Norm Todd's door — The Daily Capper said it received a message that was later obtained by Fleishman and published on the news site

HyperVocal.com that revealed much of how the capper world works.

It was from a throwaway account with the name kodypwned. If you're unaware, pwned is a popular internet slang term that derives from an old Japanese video game that misspelled the word "owned" and means decisively or humiliatingly beaten. The note is written in a manner that is often used in corners of the internet that include 4chan and similar sites, using symbols, jargon and shorthand references to internet phenomena. It read:

> Ohai thur :3
>
> I just got full dox of kody1206 (blackmailer of many like peyton, amanda, blahblahblah), Kody Maxson.
>
> [a link to an image-sharing site]
>
> dedicate a huge portion of 1 of your shows to him and the details in that pic. will get lots of attention, other blackmailers blackmailing him cos they hate him and eventually a lulzy arrest :3
>
> kbai :D

Perhaps a translation is in order. "Ohai thur" and "kbai" are slang terms meaning "oh, hi there" and "'K, bye," that originated with a popular internet meme that centered around a fat cat who is said to love cheeseburgers. The ":3" symbol is also associated with the same cat (he was very popular at the time), and is a sort of happy face. "Full dox" comes from full documentation, and in this setting generally refers to links or images that identify someone who has made an attempt to be anonymous online. And "lulzy" means laughable or amusing.

Following the link even as I write this shows a photo collage with text; it reads (the original was in all caps, but I have saved the reader from that annoyance):

> Dox of blackmailer, hacker, pedophile Kody1206 (real name Kody Maxson)

For a while now I tried to get personal info on Kody1206, for the lulz and I reached my goal, which I will share with you mentalgen.

Below you will see how I got it and how it is all connected, all info is legit.

I heard that the best way to get in touch with this blackmailer was by approaching one of the girls he is blackmailing and threatening them, because he then tries to hack and scare you.

So I contacted the one he has been blackmailing the longest, Amanda Michelle Todd, now 13 yr old camhoe from Port Coquitlam BC Canada, which he has been blackmailing for 2 years now, yes she was 11, with what?

[link to a notorious photo- and video-sharing site that no longer works]

I contacted her on her Skype Cutiielover or AmandaHatesYou and YouTube threatening her like a total newb and asking for her MSN, so she got in touch with white night blackmailer Kody and then said this is my MSN Kody@hotmail.ca, lulz, that was easy.

[picture of what appears to be a screen-cap of Amanda using the isabella00555 email account to provide the Kody1206 address]

So I am thinking, this fag being a hacker, it will be difficult info, but let's Google his email anyway, I am lazy today :3

[picture of a screen cap of a Google search of the email address and a link to a video game site called Unrealskill.com]

Oh daaaaaaamn shit just got real yo

Immediately his email is connected to the nick he uses to blackmail with and has multiple accounts with, be it gaming sites, hacking sites, porn sites different forums, just Google it yourself.

Below that are screen caps of Google searches of the name Kody1206.

So Im like this guy is a dumbass, maybe search his Facebook and Twitter with his email?

Under that are screen caps showing accounts on Facebook, Twitter, TinyChat, 4chan and other sites with the names

Kody1206 or Kody Maxson. And finally there is a Google
StreetView image of a small house with an address in New
Westminster B.C.

KBAI :3

If this email is real, and sincere, the sender not only accuses
Kody Maxson — who he says lives close to Amanda in the greater
Vancouver area — of being a blackmailer, but also admits to being
a blackmailer himself.

It also asserts, with picture evidence, that Amanda and Maxson
knew each other.

***

Another well-respected online journalist, Patrick McGuire of
Vice.com, uncovered a Daily Capper Awards video that was posted
to YouTube on December 19, 2010 — two days after Amanda had
been banned from BlogTV — and has since been taken down. At 1:19
into the video, it announces: "Amanda has been blocked a few times
for showing... she said she has been IP banned from BlogTV."

IP banning is the most serious form of punishment a website
can administer; it means it will not accept any posts from the user's
computer (every device that can access the internet has a
recognizable IP address), no matter what the account's name. It
helps prevent users from just changing their identities to get around
account bans.

As with anything that mentions Amanda, the video received
hundreds of comments. Because of The Daily Capper's security
settings, the account's owner was allowed to see the comments as
they arrived and have the choice of whether to approve them or not.
Only the approved comments would appear under the video. One of
them, shared with Fleishman, came from the isabella00555 account
and was dated January 4, 2011 — Amanda's first day back at school
after the flashing pictures were distributed to her friends and
classmates. It read:

"its amanda here, ah i am getting black mailed and the cops are out looking for the guy that posted the video of me flashing to all my family members and friends because i didn't do stuff with him on cam. put that in ur news ;) people are also getting charged but the site is shut down."

Many people, especially young ones, believe the police have powers and abilities far beyond those that they actually have. Crimes are rarely solved the way they are on TV and movies, and co-operation from victims and witnesses is absolutely vital for successful police work. If Todd could not provide specific information as to who she believed was extorting her, local police would have little chance of charging anyone with anything. They would have to hand the case to a force with more sophisticated technology and methods. And the site, if it's the one mentioned the kodypwned email, is still operating as I write this.

At the time, the RCMP made no meaningful headway into the identity of Amanda's tormenter.

At school, the bullying became so intense that Amanda switched to a new one in hopes of a new start. From Westview, she moved to Maple Ridge Secondary. It's a much bigger and more diverse school than Westview, and is known for both its academics and athletics. In fact, in the Fraser Institute's overall ranking of Canadian high schools at the time Amanda attended them, Maple Ridge scored a 6.8 out of 10 (201st in the nation), double Westview's score of 3.4.

But the tormentor found her again. According to the CBC, Amanda was tracked down again in the spring of 2011. She went to her mother, who informed the police.

At that point, the CBC and others report, Carol Todd felt as though the police were not taking the case seriously. It's not hard to understand why.

Clearly, several serious crimes had been committed against her daughter. It's immaterial whether Amanda was a willing participant in the online flash or not; capturing the image would be defined in most jurisdictions as the creation of child pornography — and it should be noted that toplessness is not illegal for Canadian women of any age. But trading, selling or posting any image of a minor containing nudity constitutes the distribution of child pornography. And, certainly, threatening to post any image unless requests for sexual favors are granted leaves the alleged tormentor liable to charges of extortion, sexual luring and sexual interference with a minor.

Although well-protected computer trails can be difficult to follow, they are hardly impossible. Even a couple of well-directed Google searches at the time could have yielded some valuable results.

That does not necessarily mean that the police were unwilling to help. Many in law enforcement, especially at the local level, are not nearly as technologically proficient as the people they are trying to investigate, and can often be overworked. Tracking an online extortionist, who could be anywhere in the world, is immensely difficult even for large law enforcement organizations dedicated to such things, let alone a small suburban RCMP detachment.

But to many — including another respected journalist, Krissy Darch, who wrote about the issue for the Vancouver Observer — the lack of law enforcement results smacked of sexism. As would become evident later, many people were quick to decide that the whole issue wasn't a big deal or that Amanda was actually to blame for the crimes committed against her, and it's hard to believe that did not include people in law enforcement as well. Besides, with the picture already out, what leverage did the extortionist have left?

Although he appears to have been unsuccessful in coercing Amanda into any of the "shows" he demanded, the person she knew as Tyler Boo continued to act. Perhaps in hopes that increased pressure would yield results or just out of anger, he allegedly, according to the CBC and other sources, sent the flashing image to students and teachers at Amanda's new school.

According to her own account, the bullying started all over again. The students at Maple Ridge were just as prone to taunt her

— labelling her "camwhore and "slut" — as the Westview kids were. Because of the torment suffered at the hands of her classmates, Amanda went through the classic signs of depression, resorting to drinking, drugs and even self-mutilation. Her parents sought help, getting her appointments with a mental-health counsellor and a prescription for antidepressants.

But it was too much for her. In September 2011, Amanda moved out of Norm's Maple Ridge house and into Carol's Port Coquitlam home so that she could change schools again. Her options were limited because her already shaky schoolwork had been seriously affected by the stress she had been experiencing and the high number of classes she had missed.

She enrolled in C.A.B.E. Secondary in Coquitlam. Intended for about 70 to 80 students who encounter problems in traditional high school setting — it features flexible schedules, youth workers who specialize in helping young mothers, and First Nations students' needs and online learning. As one Maple Ridge student told me: "C.A.B.E. is like the last-chance school; when people she you go there, they know you've been in some kind of trouble — but it's better than quitting school, eh?"

The new school didn't make a difference. In October of 2011, a month into her stay at C.A.B.E. and just short of her 15th birthday, according to the CBC, Amanda had a conversation her tormentor on Facebook in which his intentions are clearly stated:

TYLER BOO: sup camwhore, been a while :P i didnt send the video the last time because i liked how you whined,but as you know i have your new school, new schoolmates new flash your parents havent seen etc blahblah you know the drill. so 3 shows of 15 minutes and then i wont send :3

AMANDA: Oh yeah what are some names;)

TYLER BOO: lol, u already forgot who i am? the guy who last year made you change school. got your door kicked in with cops in the morning :P and also on youtube like 6 months ago whatever, scared you a bit :P you promised the authorities not to do be sexual on cam again because you are underage and it is considered producing of child porn....well, you have. so i can send them that and make them come to you again, send your new school and friends and family again. you will go through the exact same thing all over. or you can give me 3 shows and i will disappear forever. you know i wont stop until you give me those 3 shows. if u go to a new school, new bf, new friends, new whatever, i will be there again :P i am crazy yes xD so your answer :3

Despite his threats, Todd refused to give in. She responded defiantly, refusing to give into his demands.

AMANDA: do u wanna meet me ? come meet me right now.

TYLER BOO: are u drunk? xD

AMANDA: NOPE. im sober, or are u to scared fucking pedo

TYLER BOO: year scared of u and flying 3 hours.

AMANDA: ur scared of airplanes eh ?

TYLER BOO: so about them 3 shows :3

AMANDA: not gonna happen prick. so far how many people have inboxed u about this eh ?of my friends

Chapter 5: Torment

Although lots of people now claim online to have been Amanda's friend or even best friend, according to her own account, nobody at the time acted like it. When she wasn't being mocked or laughed at any of her three high schools, Amanda was being ignored. While formerly gregarious, even popular, she found herself walking to and from school alone and eating lunch alone in the school library.

Social media was no better. She was shunned there too when she wasn't being abused. In fact, the profile picture on the Tyler Boo Facebook page had been changed to her flashing picture.

Amanda showed serious signs of depression. She had a hard time getting out of bed. She started drinking and taking drugs. She even resorted to self-mutilation.

Just when all seemed lost, she got a message on Facebook. It was from "an old guy friend" from Westview, her old high school. They had always gotten along, and when he sent her encouraging messages, pointing out that he had always really liked her, she was delighted. Finally, there was someone who was not judging her for what she had done.

He told her to come over to his place, so they could "hook up."

She pointed out that she knew he had a girlfriend.

He told her that his girlfriend was away on vacation.

Amanda went to the boy's house, and they had sex. He did not message or text her again.

One picture of what many have identified as the boy in question kissing Amanda on the forehead still shows up on one of the many memorial pages on Facebook. Lots of people have asked for it to be taken down, and others have implored commenters not to "rat." A comment on the photo from Carol Todd's account reads: "Yes, I would like the pics to go. Sad memories of what wasn't right."

Word of the tryst spread rapidly. And Amanda — who was already widely regarded in her peer group as a "whore" and "slut" because of her flashing pictures — drew the ire of many girls in several high schools.

According to Amanda's own account, not long after, she was at school when she received a text from an unknown number telling her to leave school. Once outside, she was confronted by a group of more than a dozen girls, led by the girlfriend of the boy who she'd had sex with. Quickly, a crowd of kids gathered in the schoolyard.

After a few taunts and much encouragement from the crowd, the girlfriend punched Amanda, knocking her to the ground. She then leapt on Amanda, and other girls joined in on the beating.

Several of the kids watching filmed the beating on their phones. Videos of it circulated between them and others online for weeks.

No teachers or other adults seemed to be around. Certainly none intervened until after Amanda said she had been assaulted by several people and left in a ditch.

Some people have told me that Amanda's version of events contains some inaccuracies. I have been told that the incident took place inside the school, and that it was more of a fight between the aggrieved girl and Amanda — some claim Amanda even had the upper hand before other girls joined in.

I've also been told they stopped when a parent started yelling at them from inside a car and I've been told they stopped when a teacher showed up, but either way, they left behind a badly beaten young girl.

Norm Todd, who arrived to pick up Amanda at the time she normally left school, found her bruised and disoriented. He asked what happened and if she needed help. She said she would be okay.

***

Faced with a tormentor who wouldn't go away and seemed to be above the law, and constant bullying at school that had evolved into a group assault, Amanda must have felt powerless. She was in what must have appeared to be a lose-lose situation that appeared as though it would never end.

The two questions that come up most often when people talk about the case are: a) why weren't the authorities able to do something sooner? and b) why did she flash anyway? They both require complicated answers.

As far as police investigations into such cases are concerned, the people involved face a frustrating, uphill battle. Those people creating and trading in illegal images work very hard to avoid detection, and are often several steps ahead of police when it comes to technical prowess. Just as important, they are often not in the same jurisdiction as their victim or victims, making investigations exponentially more difficult. And the numbers of images and videos available have become so large that police are often overwhelmed and face a difficult process of triage when it comes to which cases to investigate.

Statistics aside, the situation facing opponents of online exploitation of children is best illustrated by a brush with the community experienced by someone I know.

I can't use his name (for reasons that will become obvious later), so let's call him David. Based in Los Angeles, David is one of the most respected investigative journalists in America. His work has solved crimes, toppled corrupt organizations and generally exposed a great deal of injustice and sleaze.

For years, he has received the help of a small-time criminal turned private investigator we'll call Jimbo. Back in the late 1990s, before Google had even registered as a company, a man walked into Jimbo's Los Angeles office and offered him money to check the background of a name he'd written down on a piece of paper.

Jimbo did a diligent job and determined that the name was actually a pseudonym for the man who had hired him. When he presented his findings to his client (who we'll call Raymond), he was delighted. Because Jimbo had done such a good job, Raymond hired him for more work.

Some weeks later, Jimbo was helping Raymond install a video surveillance system in his luxurious house (including hidden cameras in the bedroom ceilings) when Raymond asked him if he wanted any lunch. Jimbo declined, so Raymond excused himself and left for a nearby fast-food outlet. While Raymond claimed to be a humble concert promoter, Jimbo had heard that he actually made most of his money as a pimp, supplying girls to clients in L.A. and beyond. Hoping to find some names, numbers and maybe a few salacious details about Raymond's clients, Jimbo copied the contents of his laptop onto his own. He finished just seconds before Raymond returned with his food.

That night, Jimbo took a look at his spoils and was shocked by what he saw. He described it as "real sick shit." There were photos and videos of children, some very young, nude and, in some cases, having sex. Some of the images portrayed indicated acts of sexual violence against the children. He was immediately aware that what he possessed was illegal and potentially trouble for him, as well as strong evidence that Raymond was more than just a small-time pimp.

Not sure what to do, Jimbo called David the investigative journalist. David saw some of the pictures and video. Although he was relieved to see no evidence that Raymond was a participant in any of the images, he knew that his possession of them was a strong indication he was a pretty bad dude. He convinced Jimbo to take the evidence to the FBI, and agreed to go along with him for moral support.

The FBI accepted the evidence and began an investigation. A few weeks later, David learned that Raymond had been arrested in Cuba. Although Raymond later claimed it was for solicitation, David's own sources told him it was because he was trying to smuggle underage girls out of the country.

Raymond was sentenced to 10 years, and David called the FBI to tell them. He was unsurprised to learn that they decided to put Raymond's case aside for more pressing concerns.

When Raymond was eventually released from Cuba, David called the FBI again, urging them to reopen the case. They did not, but they did allow him to view the evidence so that he could write an article about the situation.

When Raymond saw the article on David's website, he immediately launched a defamation lawsuit. David told me that Raymond's lawyer called him and told him that if he could prove that Raymond was in possession of child pornography, he, as a father, would drop the suit on moral grounds. Relieved, David said he took the lawyer to the FBI's evidence room, and they showed him the pictures and videos. The lawyer, looking quite stricken, told David that as a concerned parent, he'd drop the suit immediately.

But that's not what happened. The lawyer had used David's eagerness to prove his point to force discovery. He then informed David that the suit would continue.

Although he maintains he was correct in his claims, David did not have the resources to fight the far wealthier Raymond in a prolonged suit, and the fact that Jimbo had acquired the evidence illegally made it even more complicated. Bitterly, David agreed to settle. In exchange for having the article being dropped from his website, removed from an as-of-then-unpublished book and an agreement to never write about Raymond again, David says the lawyer agreed to drop the suit. Honestly and in writing this time. So David agreed.

Frustrated and angry, David approached the FBI agent who was handling the case, and asked him why they didn't pursue charges against Raymond even though the evidence was clear and in their very hands. David told me that the agent, years of disappointment obvious on his face, told him: "I've got a hundred thousand images coming in from Estonia every day; I just don't have time for him."

It's true, law enforcement agencies are overwhelmed not just by the sheer volume of child exploitation, but also the number of people involved. With their comparatively meager resources and personnel, they are forced to pick and choose their battles. Like the narcotics cop who allows the street-level dealer to walk if it'll lead to a shot at his supplier, law enforcement officers dedicated to fighting child exploitation are primarily focused on people who makers, import and distribute illegal media, and very rarely on mere possessors.

Part of the problem is the international nature of the crime. Not only do police forces have to co-operate with those in other countries, but they have to deal with the fact that laws regarding child pornography, and its very definition, can vary wildly from nation to nation. In fact, possession of child pornography for private use is not illegal in Japan and Russia (both G8 members) and, according to the UN, 90 of its 193 member states. All pornography featuring people aged 14 and older was legal in Germany until 2008.

And law enforcement's job has been made exponentially harder because the face of child exploitation has changed. That change, like so many in our culture, has been predicated by technology.

A few generations ago, pornography (to use a politically charged, but essentially accurate term) was rare and hard to get in Western cultures. Until the controversial advent of Playboy in December 1953, images of nude and even semi-nude women were limited to high or Avant garde art or to underground publications and individual images collected and traded under a veil of secrecy.

For the most part, pornography was illegal in the West. Some publications — mostly European — dodged the law by presenting nudes as artistic photography, scientific studies of anatomy or an exploration of "naturism" (what we'd now call nudism, the lives of people who would prefer to be nude). But they were rare in North America, expensive and liable to be confiscated at port of entry by the postal service or even by police if they encountered them.

The major alternative of the pre-Playboy era was the Tijuana Bible or Eight-Pager. These were comic books with cartoon depictions of nudity and sex acts. Often poorly drawn, Tijuana Bibles usually featured celebrities of the day or mainstream cartoon characters like Blondie and Dagwood Bumstead. They were wallet-sized, easy to conceal, and extremely popular. Despite their name, and the fact that many claimed to have originated in Cuba (although Tijuana, of course, is in Mexico), most were printed in New York City. Because they were illegal, Tijuana Bibles were anonymous or attributed to artists with suggestive synonyms like "Iva Clapp."

World War II had a profound effect on pornography, as it did most of Western culture. With millions of men away from their homes, the concept of looking at images of women's bodies for sexual pleasure lost much of its stigma. Although nudity in media was still relegated (and regulated) to the underground market, portrayals of scantily clad, sexually suggestive women — which acquired the name "pinups" because soldiers would often pin them to walls for better hands-free viewing — became commonplace, even ubiquitous.

A few years later, Playboy and its subsequent imitators broke the nudity barrier. Sort of. At their onset, popular "girlie" magazines limited themselves to the exposure of breasts and other body parts, but made it a point to keep depictions of genitals and pubic hair obscured. This practice was the result of a widespread belief that although depictions of breasts and nipples had been deemed acceptable by the public at large, anything more might lead to big trouble.

But competition (and changing mores) put an end to that. Facing his first truly strong competition from a then-British-based magazine called Penthouse in the late 1960s, Playboy founder Hugh

Hefner found himself in the midst of what he called the "Pubic Wars." Both magazines began to push the limits of acceptability by publishing more and more explicit photos. It was actually Playboy and not Penthouse (as is commonly believed) that published the first mainstream photo including pubic hair in August 1969. That was followed by full-frontal nudity in January 1972.

After that, mainstream girlie magazines kept upping the ante, resorting to images of masturbation, even urination (notably, in Penthouse) before Hustler — whose owner, Larry Flynt, prided himself on pushing societal norms — began publishing images of penetrative sex, which soon acquired the name hardcore pornography, in its pages.

Moving pictures were little different. Nudity was rare in early feature films, but suggested sexuality was commonplace. Under pressure from activist groups like the Catholic Legion of Decency, Hollywood enacted the Hays Code in 1934. Under it, many moral rules — ranging from depicting any religion in an unfavorable light to showing sympathy for criminals — were banned from feature films. Some small-time producers sidestepped the ban by producing documentaries about nudists and "native tribes," but they were in very light distribution because of the ever-present threat of public outrage.

As was the case with Tijuana Bibles, a market for clandestine pornographic films emerged. People who owned home projectors could generally find someone with nude or even hardcore 8 mm films if they looked hard enough. These films — known as "stags" because they were often played at all-male parties — were usually treasured by their owners due to their rarity and illegality, and were actively if tacitly collected and traded among friends.

Attitudes began to change in the 1950s, helped along when the popular Kinsey Reports on Human Sexuality were released in 1948 and 1953, leading to an increase of discussion on sexual habits in the mainstream. Cracks appeared in the Hays Code, and in 1954 it was challenged in a New York court by the producers of Garden of Eden. The judge ruled that the film — about a young woman who fled a tyrannical father and found happiness in a nudist colony — represented an authentic lifestyle choice, paving the way for wide release. Ironically, one of the actresses who was in the film — 20 years old and married — was denied access to a showing in Tampa, Florida, because it was limited to an "adults only" audience.

The Hays Code looked hopelessly out of date by 1955 when its proponents demanded ridiculous changes to the film adaptation of Nelson Algren's classic novel, The Man with the Golden Arm, because they believed it glamorized drug use. A widespread popular backlash led to some revisions in the Hays Code, but no movement on the ban on nudity.

That ban was challenged in 1959 when former World War II combat cameraman and Playboy photographer Russ Meyer released The Immoral Mr. Teas. An endearingly cheap comedy about a nebbish-y guy who acquires the ability to see though (somehow, only women's) clothes, it was the first feature film to contain nudity that did not use nudism or some other lame excuse as a mitigating factor. In an effort to pre-empt any argument about the legality of the film, Meyer cited the 1957 decision on Garden of Eden that ruled that nudity in and of itself was not obscene. Because Mr. Teas does not get involved with the nude women around him in a sexual way (in fact, he seems to consider his new powers something of a nuisance), it was deemed permissible.

What followed was a flood of movies that featured female nudity, but no sex — a popular genre called the "nudie-cutie." But by 1964, there were so many of them competing for a limited audience — while no longer banned, nudie-cuties were generally shown only to small audiences in run-down, out-of-the-way theaters called "grindhouses" — that a new genre emerged. "Roughies," films that featured nudity and violence (but still no sex), began to dominate grindhouse screens.

One stag film maker — an aristocratic Italian named Lasse Braun who kept changing his nationality and name to avoid arrest — grew tired of the format, and started to make high-quality short films featuring nudity and sex. These shorts were distributed around the world and made a new format, the peep show, popular.

In Denmark, largely because of Braun's films, the government lifted all bans on pornography early in 1969. Later that year, the Netherlands, where Braun had settled, followed suit. Over the next few years, many feature films made in those countries contained nudity and even non-simulated sex, some including the countries' biggest stars.

Under pressure from foreign films (in which nudity had become commonplace), things started to change in Hollywood. Slowly at first. The first English-language mainstream film to show female nudity was Peeping Tom, a British horror film released in 1960. In it, model Pamela Green exposed one breast very briefly. The movie was widely panned, and Green's career was reduced to more nudist films and nudie-cuties.

It wasn't until 1963 when Jayne Mansfield appeared topless in Promises, Promises that an American mainstream actress did a nude scene or that an English-language film that nudity enjoyed wide release and commercial success. After that, a deluge of big-screen movies featured female nudity (at least toplessness). They drew the ire of groups like the Legion of Decency, but by that time the group had been pushed to the fringe, and had little sway with the public at large. The Hays Code was scrapped in 1967, and replaced by the MPAA's voluntary ratings system in 1968.

In 1969, Midnight Cowboy famously became the first mainstream film with the MPAA's harshest rating, X, to win an Academy Award for Best Picture. But the rating was due not to nudity or sex, but to its "homosexual frame of reference" and "possible influence upon youngsters," according to the MPAA.

Hardcore pornography did not arrive in mainstream theaters until 1970 when Mona, the Virgin Nymph was released. It sparked a brief period in which movies that featured hardcore porn — like 1972's Deep Throat and Behind the Green Door and 1973's The Devil in Miss Jones — were fashionable among bohemian types in the U.S. That was what many considered the golden era of porn, launching stars and establishing a parallel film community alongside Hollywood's. The era is effectively and accurately parodied in the mainstream 1997 film Boogie Nights.

But that period did not last long. Although the precedent had been broken on hardcore porn, it was not accepted (with very few exceptions) in mainstream cinema. Instead, it retreated back to the grindhouses, although to much wider audiences.

But the game changed in the early 1980s with the introduction of home video players and recorders. Home video players — called video cassette recorders or VCRs, even though many only played and did not record — became very popular in 1982, spawning the emergence of movie rental chains.

Because of the comparative anonymity allowed by home video — chains stores had "adult" sections, there were adult-only stores and porn cassettes were available by mail-order, which made viewing far less visible and dangerous than visiting a grindhouse — the porn industry expanded like a mushroom cloud virtually overnight. In 1975, the hardcore porn film industry saw revenues of about $5 million worldwide, by the middle 1990s, it had ballooned to about $13 billion in the U.S. alone. The grindhouse effectively died — most of the few that remained catered to a gay audience who prized anonymous hookups more than the action on the screen — as porn came home to stay.

At the time, two video cassette formats were widely available — Sony's Betamax and JVC's VHS. Sony refused to allow hardcore producers to use Betamax, while JVC had no such qualms. Although Beta cassettes were smaller, more reliable and generally considered to reproduce a better picture and sound, the demand for porn led its share of the home market to shrink from virtually 100 percent in 1977 to 25 percent in 1981 to 7.5 percent in 1986 and virtually zero soon after that.

Porn was suddenly huge. Not quite mainstream, but incredibly popular. It still had its opponents, though, as many people believed that paying people for sex constituted prostitution, whether it was in front of a camera or not.

In September 1983, a producer named Hal Freeman rented the Rancho Palos Verdes, California, home of an acquaintance named Nancy Conger to shoot a video called Caught From Behind, Part 2. He hired several actors, including five women (he had intended to hire six, but Conger volunteered to be in the film) from a Los Angeles talent agency, informing each of them that they would be expected to perform vaginal, oral and anal sex as part of their job.

The film set was raided, and Freeman was arrested. In a move that seems alarmingly sexist in retrospect, he was charged with five counts of pandering (pimping) under the belief that the women paid for sex were acting as prostitutes and the men paid for sex were not (and Conger was deemed to be under another classification altogether).

Despite the fact that the hardcore porn industry was thriving (Freeman himself had directed more than 100 titles by that time), he was actually found guilty, sentenced to 90 days in prison with five years' probation and slapped with a $10,000 fine. The court of appeals maintained his conviction. Although very, very few cases are overturned at that level, Freeman's lawyers approached the California Supreme Court.

After much deliberation, the court decided that since the goings-on in Conger's house were not visible to neighbors or passersby, that the video was distributed through nationally policed channels and that Freeman had not been charged with obscenity, that what he was working on was valid work of artistic expression and not prostitution.

The legal tribulations cost Freeman $300,000, but it set him free and guaranteed his and every other American the right to make hardcore pornographic films.

But there was another major complication. In 1984, an actress named Nora Kuzma took the porn industry by storm under the pseudonym Traci Lords. Beginning at just 16, (aided by a fake birth certificate acquired from her stepfather/manager), Lords performed in as many as 80 hardcore films before she turned 18. "For me, porn was about my pain in my life as a child; and I was completely acting out," Lords said years later. "I was a wild kid. I was angry at the world; and I was very rebellious, and I wanted to show everybody."

The federal government charged the producers of several of her films with child pornography, but could not make any charges stick because the producers' defense was that they had been fooled by the fake birth certificate in much the same way that the federal government had itself been fooled by her fake passport when she traveled to Paris for a shoot.

The Lords controversy prompted the U.S. government to pass the Child Protection and Obscenity Enforcement Act in 1988. Better known as 2257 regulations, the law requires all producers of commercial sexually explicit material to obtain proof that every participant is at least 18 years old, and to retain the proof (or copies thereof). Federal officials can ask for that proof at any time and any deficiency in record keeping can be met with large fines or even prison terms.

But that only applied to commercial productions. At about the same time that VCRs became popular, so did personal video cameras (known then as camcorders). Because they recorded directly to tapes that could be played in the VCR, they allowed users a level of privacy unprecedented in mainstream video culture. Before the camcorder, homemade images had to be developed, almost always by a third party who would at the very least see your pictures or films and could very well copy them for their own purposes or report them to authorities. The only exception at the time came in the form of Polaroid cameras, which self-developed. Despite poor picture quality, Polaroid quickly acquired a reputation as being preferred by home pornographers.

Free from the bonds of the developer, amateur and homemade porn took off. Before long, "amateur" videos (many of them were faked) became a thriving subset of the porn industry.

A few years after the VCR/camcorder boom, the internet changed the cultural landscape again. Ordinary people suddenly had essentially the entire collection of humankind's knowledge and accomplishment at their fingertips. It should surprise only the most naive that a huge proportion of internet traffic was dedicated to porn. Although 2010 estimates by Forbes magazine put the number of sites dedicated to porn at between 8 and 13 percent, the amount of traffic they see is enormous, accounting for about a third of all internet views. Incredibly, in 2008, Nielson reported that about a quarter of all U.S. office employees access pornography at work. As Frank Rich wrote in The New York Times Magazine: "Porn is no longer a sideshow to the mainstream. It is the mainstream."

Porn was literally everywhere, usually for free. While earlier generations of boys had to try to get their hands on Tijuana Bibles, Playboys or porn DVDs to access images of nude women or sex, all they needed after the internet boom was a computer, video game console or smartphone.

That availability led many to believe that boys were losing their ambition to pursue the attention of real girls. While it's been indicated that the women who appear in porn generally have higher self-esteem than most women, girls — their self-esteem already damaged by competing with the attractive, uncomplicated and undemanding models presented to boys in porn can be adversely affected. Many began to dress and behave more provocatively to regain lost attention. While many criticized performers of the era like Britney Spears for influencing how girls dressed and behaved, it's probably closer to the truth that Spears and her peers were more influenced by the fashions of contemporary girls rather than the other way around.

There were, however, some other media factors that did have direct effects on the sexual culture of teenage girls — sex tapes, cam girls and Girls Gone Wild.

The evolution of the celebrity sex tape was quick and clear. In 1988, during the VCR/camcorder era, a leaked videotape featuring actor Rob Lowe having sex with two young women nearly wrecked his career. But in 2001, well into the internet era, a video showing socialite Paris Hilton having sex with her boyfriend transformed her from a struggling and largely unknown model into a household name. After Hilton's success, several other women — most notably Kim Kardashian — parlayed appearances in sex tapes leaked (in some cases intentionally) to the media into mainstream careers.

The cam girl concept was launched in 1996 by a conceptual artist named Jennifer Ringley. A 19-year-old college junior, she decided to broadcast every part of her life online and she launched JenniCam.com. At first she blacked out certain moments, but eventually she showed herself nude and having sex. Her site was a huge success, attracting as many as four million viewers a day. She achieved a great deal of mainstream attention — Ringley was covered in the Wall Street Journal, appeared on Late Night with David Letterman and even played a fictionalized version of herself on a popular TV show — and managed to make a decent living at it.

JenniCam launched countless imitators. Young women, and a few young men, found it financially rewarding to broadcast themselves online. Not surprisingly, those who showed more nudity and sex had bigger, more generous audiences. The easy money attracted porn companies who paid models to strip and perform on camera for subscribers. And it also showed a generation of girls that praise and attention (and potentially cash) could come from appearing sexy online.

And a year after JenniCam debuted, an ambitious Californian named Joe Francis launched Girls Gone Wild — a series of videos that featured girls voluntarily and usually publicly exposing their breasts on camera. It was a huge success.

It wasn't actually a new idea. In the 1970s, a self-appointed sexual revolutionary named George Urban roamed the streets of New York, encouraging women to flash or strip and putting the results on Manhattan's no-holds-barred public access cable television channel on a show called Ugly George. Later, videos of women baring their breasts at Mardi Gras celebrations in New Orleans — an old tradition — were traded and sold, mainly over the internet.

But what set Girls Gone Wild apart, making it both a success and a cultural turning point, was that it was advertised, almost constantly after a certain hour, on mainstream TV. The ads showed dozens of girls, all appearing to sincerely having a great time, exposing their breasts (edited for television, of course) to throngs of appreciating fans. Not only did the ads show the girls appearing to be having the times of their lives and receiving huge amounts of attention and praise (with no visible negative consequences), it seemed like everyone was doing it. There were so many girls doing it on the commercials and the ads were so frequent that it almost appeared as though girls who were not flashing were a prudish minority. The situation was frequently satirized in movies and TV.

These forces came together to create a vortex of new sexual cultural cues for girls. They had to compete with the effortless allure of internet porn for boys' attention, they were taught they could get attention and praise by exposing their breasts and they were given the technology to do so in front of a large audience with what many believed was anonymity.

But girls knew that by exposing too much, they invited a different kind of attention. Flashing your breasts at school would definitely get the attention of the boys, but it would also give you a reputation as a slut. And that's more than an annoyance, inviting scorn from many and emboldening some potential tormentors into action. While it's absurd to blame the victim in sexual violence, the belief among girls is that to have a reputation as being sexually available or indiscriminate is to expose oneself to a higher potential for unwanted advances.

Online flashing is not entirely uncommon among Amanda's generation. There are dozens of websites dedicated to trading captures of flashes and even a phenomenon called the Anti-Boredom Game (or the Omegle Game after the website on which is was developed and popularized) in which girls are given points for how much they show and do. High scores are published online, and girls are encouraged to break previous records.

One young woman told me that she masturbated for an online audience on 4chan shortly after her 18th birthday, and — although she was aware that some would attempt to cap or record her — she was surprised when she saw her picture and video used in advertising for several online adult dating sites. Not only is she embarrassed at her youthful indiscretion, but she is unable to pursue any legal recourse without exposing herself to a wider audience, including her family. And, while she is in Canada, the sites using her image and video are mostly based in Eastern Europe.

But there are ways to expose oneself and avoid being labelled a slut. One, that Francis exploited to make Girls Gone Wild, is that people are forgiving of circumstantial behavior. It's one thing for a single woman in a crowd to flash, but if many of them do it, it seems more appropriate somehow. As one woman who appeared in a Girls Gone Wild video told me, in much the same way that a woman who would never be caught dead in a bikini on a city street has no problem wearing one at a public beach or swimming pool because it's considered culturally appropriate to do so, a college student on spring break is far more likely to flash if the practice appears to be commonplace and accepted. That was Francis' most profound effect on culture, he made flashing appear almost routine and without stigma or repercussions.

Tech advances changed things again. When Ringley started JenniCam in 1996, she had to figure out how to sync a camcorder with her computer. But just a few years later, high-quality webcams became first attachable and later built into most internet communications devices like laptops, tablets and smart phones, allowing anyone to film, record or broadcast images and videos online.

While all of that cultural history had a profound effect on Todd's life, it's very unlikely she was aware of any of it. Born in November 1996, she had never not known a world without the internet's ubiquity. She was, in fact, younger than IMDB, Amazon, eBay, Craigslist and even JenniCam. She was still in diapers when Girls Gone Wild started advertising on mainstream TV. She never lived in a world in which millions of images and video of nudity and sex were not available to anybody who with access to the internet.

By the time she flashed on BlogTV, internet pornography had become so ubiquitous that its producers had to resort to extremes to attract audiences. The situation was succinctly summed up in a Reddit interview with a hard-core porn video director who went by the name "theGreatZarquon." When asked if he watched any of his own work for enjoyment, he answered:

> "Not really. Normal porn doesn't even really get me off anymore, thanks to the internet. The hard thing about porn is that once you see enough 'normal' porn, you get bored with it. That's when I started checking out some of the weirder shit that people would send me, and it kind of snowballed from there. Now, when I watch regular porn (read: lesbian, straight or even BD/S&M), it doesn't even faze me. To put it in a nutshell, my penis has been upgraded by the internet, and it's not backwards compatible."

There was so much imagery to be had that sites needed to specialize and cater to the specific tastes of their audience. And, as we all know by now, many in that audience preferred the images of people below the legal age of consent.

Generally, media refers to all people who are attracted to minors as pedophiles, but it's not strictly true. There are three separate categories of such people widely recognized today, and they are defined by the age group they are most attracted to.

The first category — which consists of those people with an attraction to adolescents in the later stages of puberty — is clinically known as ephebophilia.

It should be understood that every time an adult who finds someone under the legally mandated age of 18 sexually appealing is not a practicing ephebophile. For example, if you see a stranger and find them attractive and then learn that they are not of age yet, it does not automatically make you an ephebophile. Instead, ephebophiles are defined as those adults who are primarily attracted to people under 18, seeking them out specifically if not exclusively.

Since the objects of ephebophilia share, in essence, the same physical characteristics as adults, many people find it relatively understandable, if not legal or tolerable. In fact, most psychologists do not even consider it a paraphilia (as unusual sexual desire, what people used to call a "perversion"), unless it interferes with the life of the patient or others.

In fact, ephebophilia was, until recently, simply considered a fact of life; looked down upon, perhaps, but certainly not despised. An excellent example is the pop song You're 16 — which contains the lyrics "You're all ribbons and curls, ooh, what a girl, Eyes that sparkle and shine. You're 16, you're beautiful and you're mine" — which became popular in 1961 when sung by 27-year-old Johnny Burnette and actually hit No. 1 when released in 1974 with 34-year-old Ringo Starr singing.

Times, of course, have changed. Teen sexuality is often quite overt in modern media, but producers are careful to keep it age appropriate. There's no way You're 16 could be released by an adult singer today, and you won't hear the existing versions on radio very often these days either.

According to my sources, the phrase among fans for porn that appeals to ephebophiles is "jailbait" or "JB." It's a widespread term used to describe an attractive teenage girl, originating in the 1930s because of the widespread belief that a statutory rape charge for sex with a partner under the age of 18 would lead to jail time.

While moral relativists can debate the implications of ephebophiles, there are far fewer who would mount any kind of defense for hebophiles. They are people attracted to a somewhat younger group than ephebophiles are. Defined by most as an attraction to people who have entered puberty, but have not come close to finishing it, hebophiles are identified as preferring people with the presence of rudimentary secondary sexual characteristics. Unlike ephebophiles, the objects of hebophiles' desires are younger-looking and not likely to be confused with adults. And hebophilia is definitely considered a paraphilia by the scientific establishment and unhealthy, even predatory, behavior by society.

And then there are true pedophiles, who are attracted to children who clearly have not yet even entered puberty. These are the boogiemen who parents around the world fear, and there really isn't anyone who would leap to their defense.

Given her young age, it would appear then, that Todd's tormentors — those who encouraged her to flash and those who extorted her for it — fit the description of hebophiles.

It's a situation that is sadly predictable. Girls, who are at least aware of a culture in which they are rewarded for nudity, are given an enhanced sense of confidence in their invulnerability by their perceived anonymity from using a pseudonym online, are encouraged by adults to show off on camera. These adults might not be all that intelligent or socially adept, but they appear make up for it with cunning, experience and ruthlessness.

And, in Todd's case, it proved disastrous.

Chapter 6: Alone

Quickly, things had gone from bad to much worse for Amanda. She had felt alone and desperate and thought she had found at least one friend in the boy who messaged her, but he turned his back on her — and she was physically assaulted for her involvement with him.

After her dad drove her home on the day of the assault, Amanda attempted suicide by drinking bleach. Not long after, Norm checked in on Amanda and found her seriously ill. He called an ambulance, and she was taken to an emergency room where they flushed the bleach from her digestive system.

After she recovered sufficiently enough to return home, she checked in on Facebook. Her page was littered with pictures of bleach and ditches tagged with her name. There were dozens of written taunts including "She deserved it, did you wash the mud out of your hair? — I hope she's dead" and "She should try a different bleach. I hope she dies this time and isn't so stupid."

It was just too much for the young girl to bear. When Amanda was well enough, she moved away from her dad's in Maple Ridge and in with her mom in Port Coquitlam, where she attended C.A.B.E.

Her parents got her help. She attended counselling and was given a prescription for antidepressants. But against the onslaught of mockery — kids from all three of her high schools were still tagging pictures of bleach with her name and calling for her to kill herself on Facebook — and pressure from her extortionist brought Amanda back to the edge.

She took an intentional overdose of antidepressants and was again revived at a hospital.

On her return home, she saw a renewed effort on Facebook to torment her.

So she made her now-famous video and put it up on YouTube.

Instead of the massive outpouring of sympathy we associate with it now, the first comments it received were taunts and further encouragement for her to kill herself.

She did. Carol Todd found her 15-year-old daughter had hanged herself in their home on October 10, 2012.

Chapter 7: Viral

After her suicide, Amanda Todd became an online sensation. Her video went viral and received tens of millions of views. The official Facebook page devoted to her memory (there were dozens of non-official ones as well), had nearly a million likes in the first few days after it was established. In December 2012, Yahoo Canada reported that hers was the third most searched for name of the year.

But as the Facebook pages were rapidly growing, it proved impossible to moderate them. Quickly they became repositories of hurtful comments, insults, jokes and even the same images that had used by the tormentor. Although most of the abusive comments and entreaties for her to kill herself that had been posted while she was still alive had been deleted by those who had posted them.

There was little that the page owners could do but delete what they considered offensive material (even illegal images), ban the poster and inform Facebook.

In fact, while the magnitude of worldwide outpouring of sympathy for Amanda was staggering, so was size of the backlash.

Literally thousands of posts on her official Facebook memorial page, her YouTube video and other sites operated by her family, friends and other well-wishers were dedicated to mocking her memory. People found it appropriate to make jokes about drinking bleach or to berate Todd for her behavior or her parents for raising such a child. It was open season on Amanda and her parents, and those doing the sniping had little if any fear of punishment.

Dozens of YouTube videos were posted, either mocking her or claiming to "tell the truth" about her, which invariably were simple, largely uninformed rants about how she got what she deserved, as though the death penalty was appropriate for online flirting.

Even more people downloaded her video — the software to download YouTube videos is available free online — then quickly re-uploaded it to YouTube with a similar title. It makes sense because YouTube pays people who upload videos that get high numbers of views. Anyone posting an Amanda Todd video at the time was essentially guaranteed a huge number of views and a potential cash windfall for a few minutes of work.

Hundreds of memes — pictures with text traded online intended to be funny or insightful — were made, many of them attempting to find humor in the concept of drinking bleach, but even more of them claiming that Amanda deserved what happened to her because of her own actions or that she deserved no sympathy because her "first world problems" were not deemed by the meme-makers to be serious enough. There was even a trending meme category that referred to teen suicide as "#todding."

Rumors, reported as fact, spread online that Todd was promiscuous, even a prostitute. Some said she and her father were in a sexual relationship. Of course, they were not true.

Literally hundreds of derogatory comments were coming into the official Amanda Todd memorial Facebook page every day. So a group of people concerned about them coalesced and began calling themselves We Are Against Bullying.

Its members started monitoring the page, cataloguing what they considered to be offensive comments and reporting them to

Facebook. The company said it had "zero tolerance" for hate speech, and the group wanted to see it act on its promise.

They had sent thousands of comments to Facebook, with no real action taken by the company. But one of the comments — which said "it's about time this bitch died" — stuck with one of the group's founders. "It made my stomach turn that someone could write that after this person had committed suicide," Christine Claveau told reporters. "It was terrible." Claveau, who'd grown up in Alberta, said that she'd been moved by Amanda's story because she too had been bullied when she was young.

So instead of just reporting the comment to Facebook, she decided to check out the personal Facebook page of the person who left it. It turned out that he was one of the rare commenters who used his real name. Claveau found out that he lived in Toronto and that he worked at a retail store called Mr. Big and Tall.

She then notified Grafton-Fraser Inc., the company that owns Mr. Big and Tall. Not long after, the man who had left the comment was fired. "We are deeply saddened by the loss of Amanda Todd," said Dave McGregor, president and CEO of Grafton-Fraser. "Out of respect for the family, I decided not to comment further on this situation beyond our statement that we took the action we felt to be appropriate. I will tell you that the individual in question is no longer employed with our company."

After that incident made the news all over the world, hundreds of people commented on social media and online news sites that the man was only exercising his freedom of speech. Perhaps, but they forgot that free speech also means that the speaker must face the response to what they have said.

By using his real name to make the comment, he — unlike many other commenters and perhaps inadvertently — took responsibility for his comment, and it got him fired.

Others called Claveau a "rat" or a "snitch."

If you're looking for Claveau on Facebook, she's still there, but she's changed her name on her account.

Interestingly, several dozen Facebook pages memorializing Amanda Todd popped up as the story about her suicide gained steam. Many of them took pictures from the official site or the news and wrote a few cursory things about Amanda.

While it's probably true that many of them were sincere expressions of sympathy, some of them appeared as though they made to generate traffic for advertising revenue, just like YouTube videos. Interspersed between images, videos and written tributes to Todd were ads for cellphones, jewelry and even performance car parts. One page — Rest In Paradise Amanda Michelle Todd, which had "likes" from 46,724 people — did not have any such ads, but that did not prevent one user from offering $5,500 U.S. for the page.

***

After Amanda had received the fourth threat, the RCMP had reacted by sending Carol Todd an email admitting their impotence and offering some advice:

> "I would highly recommend that Amanda close all her Facebook and email accounts at this time, If Amanda does not stay off the internet and/or take steps to protect herself online ... there is only so much we as the police can do."

Cold comfort; and according to many experts, a very bad idea (not to mention that it shifts both responsibility and some of the blame to the victim). Most law enforcement agencies, including the Ontario Provincial Police's integrated child exploitation unit, take a more pro-active approach. "We'll actually assume (the victims') accounts, and we'll continue chatting with an individual to try and get ourselves in a position where we can identify them and then go get them," the OPP's Det.-Sgt. Frank Goldschmidt told the CBC. "It doesn't take long for the offender to re-establish a connection through another means, whether it's another chat forum on the internet or simple email."

It seems, almost, as though the RCMP were as naïve as Amanda herself when they suggested she take such simple steps to protect herself. When their advice to her became public after her suicide, it did little to endear the RCMP to the people of the Greater Vancouver area, plenty of whom had an already low opinion of them. Many people there considered their investigation of a long list missing and murdered women — as many of 60 of them — as lackadaisical at the very least and potentially sexist and racist, and also saw them as powerless against the violent drug-fueled gang wars that had gripped the area for close to a decade.

Was there a chance that a pro-active stance by law enforcement, could it have saved Amanda's life? It's not out of the question. Although it would not have stopped the bullying she received at school, it could have relieved the feeling that she and her family were powerless to fight back at her extortionist. If the RCMP had engaged in a dialogue with her tormentor, even if it did not lead to an arrest, it could have dissuaded more threats. And Amanda no longer would have had a black cloud of a future in which she received constant threats and demands hanging over her head.

But it didn't happen.

Instead, the RCMP launched their investigation on October 11, 2012 — one day after Amanda died. Officers from two branches of the RCMP, Coquitlam and Ridge Meadows in Maple Ridge, were assigned to the case. "We will be looking into any past events that had occurred in this young girl's life, any individuals she may have been in contact with through social media, face-to-face," said Sergeant Peter Thiessen, a spokesman for the Lower Mainland District RCMP in a media release. "Anything and everything around her life, really, and what components of that may have played a role in her making this decision."

To help generate tips, they set up a difficult to remember email address — AmandaTODDinfo@rcmp-grc.gc.ca.

A different investigation was already going on. Whenever a child dies in B.C. and there are suspicious or extenuating circumstances, the body is handed over to the coroner's Child Death Review Unit.

It's a panel of experts from medical and social fields that prepare a report for the chief coroner, so that he or she might determine the next phase of action.

The massive public interest in the case and sympathy for Amanda did not go unheard by B.C. politicians. Resounding calls for tougher anti-bullying laws were answered by Premier Christie Clark in a CBC interview. "We do need to be careful about creating laws that are going to impinge on people's privacy and freedom of speech. I think that's an important principle we need to preserve as well," she said. "This situation is awful, it's tragic ... but at the same time we need to remember the solution to the problem is going to be education."

To many, that stance seemed out of character for Clark. She had long been an advocate of anti-bullying measures; just a few months earlier (in June 2012), she helped launch a series of government initiatives that provided training to help teachers and other people who work with children to detect signs of bullying and even intervene in certain situations.

Those initiatives were spurred by the death of another B.C. girl in March 2002. Dawn-Marie Wesley of Mission was 14 when her 13-year-old brother discovered her body. She had hanged herself with her dog's leash. She left a note that read (in part):

> "If I try to get help, it will get worse. They are always looking for a new person to beat up and these are the toughest girls. If I ratted, they would get expelled from school and there would be no stopping them. I love you all so much."

Of the three girls mentioned by Wesley as bullies (all former friends), two were tried and one was actually convicted of criminal harassment and uttering death threats with the intent of instilling fear.

But the Wesley case was hardly open and shut. Despite the note she left claiming that bullying had led her to kill herself, the Mission RCMP originally ruled out any suspicious activity and initially chose not to investigate, let alone lay charges. It was only after members of the community found out that one of the accused was the daughter of a Mission RCMP officer that the case was re-opened after a significant outcry.

And many saw the idea of anti-bullying laws as long overdue. B.C. public schools had been acquiring a reputation as being terrifying places, at least for some. In the same year that Wesley hanged herself, a 14-year-old Surrey boy named Hamid Nastoh jumped off a bridge with a knapsack full of rocks, killing himself and leaving behind a note blaming bullies (although not naming names), a Vancouver Island teen broadcast video of a schoolyard assault on YouTube attributed to bullies and a recent graduate sued his North Vancouver high school, claiming that it violated his human rights by not protecting him from bullies.

Anti-bullying legislation is by nature difficult because it's hard to define what bullying is and what parts of it are hurtful enough to be prohibited. In fact, most of what we call bullying is already against the law. It should be noted that the aggressors in the Wesley case were not charged with, nor convicted of, bullying. Instead, they were subject to existing laws against death threats and criminal harassment. Similarly, charges and convictions of assault have been made in cases referred to as bullying in the media.

Civil liberties advocates were against the ideas of all-inclusive bullying laws, under which name-calling could potentially become a criminal offense. While that might make sense in the setting of a high school classroom, it could also eventually allow the authorities to arrest anyone criticizing the government. As Clark pointed out, freedom of speech and privacy could be easily put into jeopardy by such laws, and such issues are more the jurisdiction of federal, not provincial, governments.

Moreover, there is a compelling argument that the anti-bullying laws would have made little if any difference in Todd's case. While it is true that her peers made life more difficult for her, the problems created by her tormentor (which precipitated the bullying) were far more profound. And what he did — extortion and distributing child pornography — were already against several existing laws. But while investigating and prosecuting a skilled capper, especially if he were determined to be in another country, would be difficult, time-consuming and expensive with little political gain, publicly stating your disapproval of bullying is cheap and can be politically fruitful.

On October 16, 2012, the RCMP issued a press release that claimed they were "sifting through thousands of tips" received through the email address they had set up. "The outpouring of support, emotion and information is literally overwhelming," said Thiessen. "The internet and social media were central to Amanda's story and they are central to our investigation as well. One of our big challenges right now, is false information that is being spread by people who appear to be trying to use Amanda's story to do harm or make a profit."

Along with the usual number of unhelpful and even malicious tips, he was alluding to the fact that a rumor had been spread that Amanda's autopsy photos were available online (they weren't, in no small part because they did not exist as no autopsy was performed), and that at least a few people had actually started making money through websites asking for donations that they claimed were going to the Todd family or anti-bullying advocacy groups. Thiessen's prepared statement was:

> "Taking advantage of a family's grief is despicable. We want to get the word out that there is one real account and anyone who is interested can make a donation at any RBC branch to the Amanda Todd Trust Account."

Chapter 8: Anonymous

While the number of views (and comments) on Amanda's YouTube video and her Facebook memorial page kept rising, other forces came into play.

One notable voice came from Anonymous, a self-appointed group of internet-based activists who claim to fight for what they see as justice without using their real identities.

A little history is in order. Back in 1999, a guy named Richard Kyanka founded a website called SomethingAwful. Although it started out as a repository for his own personal information and opinions, it quickly became popular, especially its forums, as a place for people to discuss video games and anime, among other topics. But in 2001, Kyanka announced that he would charge $9.95 for membership fees to SomethingAwful because several advertisers had reneged on their deals to pay him, and because he wanted to filter and reduce the rising number of nuisance posts his forums had been encountering.

One of the dedicated SomethingAwful users who did not want to pay the fee was a young New Yorker named Christopher Poole, who was better known to his online peers as "moot," the name he filed his posts under. In 2003, at age 15, Poole created his own site to discuss anime called 4chan. It was a simple site with no real content aside from posts of text, photos and illustrations created by its users.

4chan immediately found a following and became very popular, ranking as high as the 56th-most visited website in the world at one point. But as it grew in users, it also grew in scope. From two anime-related discussion boards at its inception, 4chan would grow several more widely varying topics (there are 63 different discussion boards on 4chan as I write this).

But the one that drew most interest was a board called /b/, which was intended for "random" posts that did not match any other category. It's actually from 4chan's /b/ that much what we know as internet culture derived. Such staples as memes, LOLcats, Rick-rolling and other standbys all actually began and were initially popularized there.

But so did a lot of porn, much of it user-generated and all of it unregulated.

In an effort to hide their identities (and many 4chan users wanted to), unsigned posts were given the name "anonymous." Before long, 4chan users began to discuss Anonymous as though it were a single entity, a person or group with a single aim.

From that amorphous beginning, Anonymous quickly took shape. Originally, the aim of Anonymous was absolute freedom of expression on the internet. But it adapted to defend the rights and interests of its users, usually by taking on perceived enemies by interfering with their websites. Bands of activists, often wearing Guy Fawkes masks (long a symbol of anti-establishment defiance and recently made more popular by the film V for Vendetta), began to assert their opinions online. People and groups claiming to be Anonymous have launched attacks on anti-piracy sites, the Church of Scientology, Westboro Baptist Church and several other online targets like PayPal and Visa. They were also instrumental in helping and organizing much of the Occupy movement.

Several Anonymous attacks have been aimed at sites that activists say contain child pornography. In 2011, Anonymous launched Operation Darklight in which it infiltrated an alleged child porn site called Lolita City, and leaked what it said were the real identities of 1,589 users, who allegedly traded illegal images on the site.

So it was to the surprise of few that Anonymous, unsolicited, became involved in the Amanda Todd case. It involved the internet, anonymity issues, injustice and even child pornography. Even more to the point, many people online considered the police to be flailing, presenting an opportunity for Anonymous to save the day and make the establishment look bad at the same time.

But there are some problems with Anonymous. If its members can remain anonymous, they are then not liable to prosecution (several alleged members of Anonymous have been arrested over the years, though, as they have not hidden their identities quite well enough) and they can act irresponsibly and illegally because of their confidence in their own invulnerability. Of course, by doling out punishments for what they believe are injustices, they are foisting their own morality, no matter what it might be, on the larger community. And, finally, by being an organization with no official membership, anyone who wants to can call themselves Anonymous, and can behave as such. The allure for a lonely internet user with delusions of being an avenging superhero is obvious.

But what first emerged from Anonymous in regard to the Todd case was puzzling to say the very least. Long thought to be sworn enemies of those who would use the internet to prey upon children, the first salvo fired by a group or individual calling themselves Anonymous came out firmly on the anti-Amanda side. In fact, in a video posted to YouTube in October 2012, someone calling themselves Anonymous claimed Amanda did not die, and that she never existed at all. Over the image of an empty suit, a heavily modified voice read the following tract:

Dear brothers and sisters.

It is now time for you to open your eyes. Some of you accused our last public announcement as fake and harsh, but we can assure you we are not fake. Nor will we stand to see our society collapse. In a publicity stunt, this mysterious figure "Amanda Todd" was denounced as dead. We are here to spread the message that there was no character called Amanda Todd. You have all been confused, lied to. As some of you may have noticed, the official page announcing her death was created on August 10th, 2012. Isn't it mysterious that this Amanda Todd passed away on October 10th, 2012? I think so, and many citizens of the world agree. The media is using this story, spreading it. Mainly for the fact to catch internet users who download and watch child pornography. You have been lied to, together we will stand to defeat the evil scheme of the media. They think they can control us, but we will not be silenced. We, as a nation, will not stand for this.

We are anonymous. We are Legion. United as ONE. Divided by zero. The media. Expect us!

Exceptionally poor grammar notwithstanding, the message is clear. Anonymous, at least this person or group using the name, was making the claim that the death of Amanda Todd was a hoax, part of a media conspiracy to find child pornography users and traders.

As evidence, they claimed to have found a Facebook page dedicated to her memory was started on August 12, 2012, but provided no evidence of it. I have been unable to uncover any other evidence to support that claim, and believe it to be spurious.

But the Amanda-is-a-hoax story had legs, and there are still people on the internet who are promoting the idea that, if she ever actually existed, she is alive and in a hospital or living under another identity.

More interesting, though, is that the video (since removed from YouTube) appears to be coming out in favor of child pornography — or at least warning its users to be careful. That's not just a very bold statement, one that flies in the face of widespread, almost universal, morality in North America, but also one that contravenes almost all of what Anonymous had worked to establish in the past.

That's the problem with groups that can't control who uses their name. The message delivered by those who call themselves Anonymous might not represent that of others who consider themselves the "real" Anonymous.

***

On October 14, 2012, the Meadow Ridge Knights — a local football team made up of high-school aged players — dedicated that day's game to Amanda's memory. The game started with a moment of silence, and the players wore pink socks in her honor. Although more closely associated with breast cancer, wearing pink has since become part and parcel of the anti-bullying movement.

The local CBC affiliate filmed the event and spoke with a few girls who said they were Amanda's friends. They were handing out pink and purple ribbons ("because we knew her favorite colors") shaped like the infinity symbols ("because she drew them everywhere"). More girls, whose identities were not broadcast, gave stock comments about how bullying's a bad thing and that "words can hurt."

While a TV news video like that would have gone unquestioned in the past, that's not how media works these days. As I write this, the video has 119,866 views. Of those viewers, 25 gave it a down vote, and 431 commented on it. Many of the comments that were not overt trolling attempts or argument starters — the first was "Have fun in hell Amanda" — were from viewers pointing out that they believed the girls in the video who claimed to be her friends were "fake" and pointed out that they seemed delighted and proud of themselves at their efforts rather than grieving or even at all upset about a friend's death.

Michael, who attended the game, did not want to speak specifically about the girls who appeared on camera, but did say that before and after the moment of silence, it was business as usual for the high schoolers who attended. "They talked shit about other kids like they always do," he told me. "They said one thing in front of the cameras and adults, and another when they were away [from them]."

Other people have come out online, claiming to be Amanda's friends on blogs, forums and other outlets like Yahoo Answers. Although they were greeted with much of the same supporting and offending comments, they also faced a new kind of commenter — those who blamed them for Amanda's death because they "didn't do anything."

Later, Michael told me: "You can say what you want and wear what you want, but you'll never stop bullying." He's right, of course, but I don't share his cynical opinion that anti-bullying campaigns are not worthwhile. Kids of his generation have grown up in a world that is far more tolerant of and less likely to have a problem with people of different ethnic origins and sexual preferences than those before them. It's not perfect, but it keeps getting better. And I attribute that in no small part to the efforts of anti-racism and anti-homophobia advocates.

But if you want to stop or even reduce bullying, you have to go to its roots — to find out why bullying happens. Hogan Sherrow, Assistant Professor of Anthropology in the Department of Sociology & Anthropology at Ohio University and the Director of the Hominid Behavior Research Project, wrote about the origins of bullying for Scientific American. He determined not only that bullying is a universal human experience found in every human culture, but that it occurs among many social animals as well, especially our closest relatives.

Bullying actually emerged as a human behavior, he and others who have studied the phenomenon say, as a defense mechanism. It originated in humans when they were still a relatively vulnerable species, prone to predation and disaster. Because any behavior outside of the norm could lead to danger — for example, when the rest of a group is being quiet to avoid detection, any loud members could put them at unnecessary risk — examples of obvious deviation from group behavior was met with censure, sometimes violently.

Of course, our society has changed a great deal since then, but — at least in some people — the need to maintain the norm by punishing outliers is still hard wired. Bullies rarely articulate to themselves why they do what they do, but when they do, they tend to justify their behavior by maintaining that they bully to "help" or "toughen up" their victims.

While that sort of logic might seem counter-intuitive, it has deep roots. But the prevailing belief among behaviorists is that it can be mitigated by the same types of education and advocacy programs that have reduced racism and homophobia.

The road seems longer for girls than boys. Slut-shaming — for want of a better term — is still a strong force in our society, demanding that girls and women be responsible for the actions of the boys and men around them. And it often has official backing.

For example, in May 2015, Lauren Wiggins, then 17 and a Grade 12 student, wore an ankle-length halter dress to her classes at Harrison Trimble High School in Moncton, New Brunswick. She was told not only that her outfit was "inappropriate," but also that it was "sexually suggestive."

She was outraged in no small part because she had frequently seen boys at the school flout the dress code with no fallout. Besides, her parents had approved of her choice of clothes and she had worn the same outfit to a successful job interview.

Wiggins fought back, on Facebook and in a letter to the school's vice-principal. In it, she wrote: "If you are truly so concerned that a boy in this school will get distracted by my upper back and shoulders, then he needs to be sent home and practice self-control." For her efforts, she received a day's suspension.

But it was under the catch-all banner of bullying, rather than the more difficult one of slut-shaming that politicians rallied around. On October 14, 2012 (the same day as the memorial football game), Dany Morin, an MP from Chicoutimi-Le Fjord in Quebec, introduced a motion in parliament to create an all-party committee to come up with a national anti-bullying plan. While no actual law was called for, the motion did spark much discussion in Parliament about bullying, particularly cyberbullying. Kerry-Lynne Findlay, a Conservative MP from Delta-Richmond East (a riding not far from Maple Ridge and Port Coquitlam) pointed out that her own daughter had recently been the victim of such online attacks and had even received death threats.

Actually, Ontario and Quebec had already passed anti-bullying laws. In fact, Ontario's came into effect on September 1, 2012, when Amanda was still alive. But it did not come easily. The Accepting Schools Act (known as Bill 13 before it was passed) was designed to make schools responsible for providing bully-free environments to all children. Liberal Premier Dalton McGuinty promoted the bill heavily and frequently invoked the names of Jamie Hubley and Mitchell Wilson, two Ontario children who had recently committed suicide after having been bullied. But the bill, popular in polls, was heavily debated because of its wording. Roman Catholic school boards opposed the bill's requirement that schools must allow anti-bullying clubs under the government-mandated name "Gay-Straight Alliance." All 65 Liberal and NDP members of provincial parliament voted for the bill, all 36 Conservatives voted against it.

It remains to be seen what effect such bills will have. But even if bullying were effectively eradicated, it would not have relieved Amanda of her worries. The threats she received from her alleged tormentor were not exactly bullying, although he did use the threat of bullying for leverage. She was, by many accounts, already bullied in school due to her learning disability. Of course, the bullying intensified to what could be described as an unbearable degree, but what her online tormentor did to her would not be described as bullying — that would be called extortion and sexual interference. From that perspective, the tormentor appears more as a sociopath than a garden variety bully. And the laws against what he did were already in place, just not being enforced.

Chapter 9: Sympathy

But while the online condolences were mounting, the real world was demonstrating sympathy too. A reporter from the Vancouver Sun visited Carol Todd's house to find a great outpouring of sadness. There were flowers on every surface of the home, and plenty of visitors. Premier Clark had dropped by (and was presented with a pink anti-bullying bracelet by Carol), as did Leah Pells, a former Olympian and Amanda's favorite teacher at C.A.B.E. Several friends came over, and shared stories and remembrances.

And Norm Todd spoke to the media for the first time. He told the reporter about when he had picked Amanda up from school the day she had been assaulted. He was shocked, he said, that the aggressors had planned the event and had waited for his daughter to be alone in the schoolyard. After the assault, he said, he found her wandering around the schoolyard, hurt. She told him that a teacher had sought to help her after the incident, but she was too distraught to accept it.

He also pointed out that Amanda and he had planned to get matching tattoos with the message "Stay Strong." Amanda had gotten the idea, he said, came from pop singer and anti-bullying advocate Demi Lovato, of whom Amanda was a big fan. Lovato revealed on Ellen, the popular daytime talk show hosted by Ellen DeGeneres, that she had been bullied so severely as a youth that she had to be home schooled, suffered from depression, an eating disorder and self-mutilation. Since then, she has been an outspoken proponent for anti-bullying organizations and has used the phrase "stay strong" as a motivator.

Significantly, Lovato appeared in Vancouver at the We Day concert on October 18, 2012. Sponsored by Free the Children, We Day is a benefit concert held annually that raises funds and awareness for children's rights around the world. Free the Children itself was the brainchild of a 12-year-old Torontonian named Craig Kielburger who decided to found the organization in 1995 after he was moved by a newspaper article about a fellow 12-year-old in Pakistan who was a virtual slave. By the time Amanda committed suicide, the organization had grown large and had become a strong advocate of anti-bullying measures.

At the concert, Lovato performed and spoke at length about her own struggles with bullying, and her desire to help stop it, but did not mention Amanda by name as many of her peers told me they had expected.

***

But while the public outpouring of sympathy for Amanda was swelling in size — the most popular of the many Facebook pages dedicated to her memory was reaching a million likes — the backlash was also firmly in place.

On October 16, 2012, a YouTuber called The Amazing Atheist posted a video called "THE AMANDA TODD SQUAD - Astonishing Moral Hypocrisy," which quickly gained hundreds of thousands of views. In it, he put forth his opinion that the worldwide sympathy for Todd was misplaced and hypocritical because there were many other children who committed suicide and were not made into posthumous celebrities, and thousands of people die every day because of other potentially preventable causes like global hunger.

While he wasn't one of the many internet trolls who simply trashed the memory of Amanda to draw attention to himself (and there were a shocking number of them), his anger at the attention paid to Todd after her death seemed to many to be displaced. The awareness raised by Todd's suicide led to funding of anti-bullying movements that would conceivably help all victims of bullying, well known or not, and it's unlikely that if the attention paid to her was redirected that would have any effect on the such complicated and age-old problems as starvation in developing nations.

***

And it was on that same day that Anonymous struck again. This time with much more significance.

Claiming to have found Amanda Todd's tormentor, someone claiming to represent Anonymous uploaded a YouTube video of a man wearing a Guy Fawkes mask with a heavily distorted voice who directed viewers to a link to a page on Pastebin.com, a popular text-sharing site.

Viewers who followed the link saw a collage that was made up of Kody Maxson's name, address and other information. Except for the inclusion of a heavily edited version of what they claimed was the original flashing picture, it was basically the same information Fleishman had received from kodypwned. The masked figure names Maxson specifically and says that he "is an abomination to our society, and will be punished."

But in a move rare for those claiming to represent Anonymous, the video's narrator actually hinted at the organization's fallibility. Addressing the idea that they could have the wrong individual, the narrator pointed out that it didn't really matter, saying: "At the most, this is the person who did this to Amanda Todd; and, at the least it's another pedophile that enjoys taking advantage of children."

The information was published, or at least alluded to, in media (both mainstream and social) all around the world almost immediately.

Anonymous also sent one mainstream media source, CTV's Vancouver affiliate, an email that read (in part):

> "We generally don't like to deal with police first hand but were compelled to put our skills to good use protecting kids. Ironically we have some good people in Vancouver who brought this to our admin's attention. It's a very sad story that affects all of us."

Reporters from CTV were actually able to track down Maxson that day, even though the address given by both kodypwned and Anonymous was incorrect (as was much of their other information). An unappealing picture of him — looking obese with one arm around a much smaller young man and his other hand holding a half-empty 40-ounce bottle of malt liquor — ran widely on mainstream and social media.

Coincidentally, the reporters said they found him on his way to Surrey Provincial Court where he was answering charges of sexual assault and sexual interference with a person under 16 in a case unrelated to Todd.

One reporter, Lisa Rossington, asked him about Amanda. The young man she identified on camera as Maxson, dressed in a black "Stompdown Killaz" hoodie, told her that he knew Amanda "in a sense" through her singing videos on YouTube and that they had communicated online, but it wasn't him who extorted or tormented her. He also said that she had reached out to him because he was a "known hacker." He then went on to say that he believed the tormentor was a capper he knew named Viper, who lived in New York, and that he had passed everything he knew about the case to the RCMP (the RCMP did not at the time acknowledge that they had received any communication from Maxson). He added: "If I was a tormentor, I'd be in police custody."

Plenty of people were more than happy to believe the masked man with the distorted voice in the video. They wanted someone to blame. And Maxson appeared to fit the bill.

Postmedia News then spoke with Maxson's mother, who refused to appear on camera. She acknowledged the charges of sex with a minor he was facing, but said he was generally a good kid. "Yeah, he has issues, like we all do — but he's not a creepy street hoodlum doing crime," she said.

She also made a plea for people to withhold judgment and to leave her son alone, noting that he was facing what amounted to a "lynch mob" that was causing all of her family anguish. Through tears, she lashed out at those who would publicly pillory her son. "It's really dangerous to throw out names when you don't know," she said. "This is doing more harm than good."

She then told the reporter that she believes her son's story that named a New York City-based capper as the culprit, and went on to claim that Kody had actually worked to out men who had visited a website with pictures of young children. She said that the people claiming to be Anonymous who named her son were actually those same people whose identities he had turned over to the authorities, and that they were naming him out of revenge.

When asked what she thought of the evidence Anonymous had posted online, she said: "Half that stuff can be doctored."

Such is the speed of media that online news services were already investigating and reporting on Maxson. Gawker — the Manhattan-based news and gossip site well known to Canadians due to its role in the Rob Ford crack-smoking story — tracked down a Reddit account named Kody1206.

Reddit is an immensely popular link- and image-posting site that is viewed by millions of people every day. It is broken down into what are known as Subreddits in which posters discuss specific topics. Gawker said that it found several posts, including pictures of young girls, from Kody1206's account on a Subreddit called Jailbait.

It was one of several controversial Subreddits started and moderated by a software developer named Michael Brutsch under the name Violentacrez. Gawker's own investigation into the 49-year-old's Reddit activity found that he also started Subreddits called Creepshot, Rapebait, Incest and Misogyny, prompting them to name him "the biggest troll on the Web" and "Reddit's creepiest user."

For their efforts, Gawker's staff were IP banned from Reddit as a freedom-of-speech movement among fellow Redditors emerged to come to Brutsch's defense. Reddit did later get rid of the Jailbait Subreddit (and several others) after they were investigated on CNN by Anderson Cooper, and Brutsch — his identity revealed — lost his job.

Later on the same day that the Anonymous video named Maxson, Gawker reported that all of the images he had posted to Reddit had since been "scrubbed" (removed). They could not determine who had deleted them, and nobody took responsibility.

At the same time, several Facebook groups dedicated to vigilante justice with names like Kody maxson WILL die (whose owner also took the mantle of Anonymous), Kody Maxson is a Murderer and Kody Maxson – We Will Find You emerged, many of them making vague threats, like recommending that Maxson "sleep with one eye open." Risking libel suits, criminal harassment charges and clearly egging on those who would use violence rather than due process, they regularly accused Maxson of being guilty and, at least figuratively, called for his head.

A typically strident and poorly crafted entry from Kody Maxson is a Murderer posted by its owner on October 17, 2012 read:

"We got almost 700 likes thanks for this support, this guys reputation and life deserve to be over and global awareness of these type of monsters is important in this digital age. There is no doubt Kody Maxon killed this girl. Tell your friends who this scumbag was and what he really did to take a life away from what could've been an innocent young beautiful girl. I weep for the world when I hear of such atrocities but here we stand united against the evil of this world. He is the embodiment of the worst kind of sinister evil possible, taking joy in the torment of a child and getting sexual gratification from it. This man could've been anyone you passed by everyday, a light has been shed on this behavior and hopefully this will be a lesson to others who engage in these disturbed an depraved activities. Kody Maxon is a true sociopath."

For his part, Maxson told CTV that he had received more than 50 emailed death threats and thousands more on Facebook.

In fact, simply standing up for due process could lead people into deep trouble. Eric Gottardi, a Vancouver-based defense attorney, was quoted in The Globe and Mail warning people not to rush to judgment. "The system isn't supposed to convict someone before charges are laid. It's not supposed to be judge, jury and executioner, all in the public forum," he said. "We have a justice system. It's supposed to work, it does work." For that, he received several angry emails, many were from people who mistakenly believed he was representing Maxson.

Much to the disappointment for those beating the anti-Maxson drums, Anonymous did not do a very good job when it came to its research, and there were several holes in their story.

The first was that they gave the wrong address. Although they were not far off in the global sense, Maxson did not and had never lived at the New Westminster house they cited. But its actual neighbors did experience some disturbance, which they attributed to anti-Maxson activists. It didn't help that a local radio station quoted an unnamed passerby as calling the address "a known party house on the weekend with lots of young women coming and going." It's a testament to how quickly news — or a facsimile thereof — travels these days in that the same quote showed up on that same day in The Daily Mail, a British newspaper.

They also erred on their target's age. Anonymous and its supporters reported Maxson's age as 30 or 32. But, as court records showed, he was 19 at the time.

And, on that same day, the RCMP reacted to Anonymous. They issued a media release, signed by Thiessen, that read:

> "Investigators spent considerable time yesterday responding to rumours spreading quickly through online and social media. One unfounded allegation involved the release of information that spread quickly online identifying a man as Amanda's tormenter."

Maxson was not charged with any offenses in relation to Amanda Todd. And his lawyer, David Gable, issued the following statement:

> "Police have announced he is a person of no interest to them regarding Amanda Todd. His thing came about through an anonymous group that hacked in through a computer and got a lot of IP addresses, his being only one of them."

Another respected online journalist, Lorraine Murphy, tracked down the person or people who outed Maxson. She saw that Twitter posts connected to the posts regarding Todd and Maxson appeared with the hashtag #OpRIP. She traced it back to a group called NJAnon. It was a smallish group, claiming about 100 members, and it had a threatening, if grammatically incorrect, slogan: "Because none of us is as cruel as all of us."

Murphy managed to get a representative of NJAnon to speak to her on Twitter, and asked about the fact that they had given the wrong address. NJAnon responded flippantly: "i knew he was in vancouver but not certain where exactly. i think its fine now though since the police know about dakota's connection to amanda." Kody Maxson's given name is Dakota.

And when she asked how they found the material they published, the response was: "lol google is more powerful then people perceive."

Later that same day, a Twitter account called Ag3nt47 identified a teenager named Alex Ramos as the person who started the rumor that autopsy photos of Amanda were online — even though the coroner said she had not undergone an autopsy. His Twitter account (@shuxbro) had its name changed to Seized by Anonymous and its subhead changed to "Respect the Dead Next Time Alex Ramos!" It still hasn't been fixed.

***

It had been quite a week since Amanda's suicide. Her memory had received the condolences and sympathy of millions online, but it had also been berated and abused by thousands. The very people who might have been her friends were said to have celebrated with a party when they heard the news that she had died. Hers became a household name, but associated almost as much with wanton, self-destructive behavior as it was with her tragic story. Anonymous had come to the rescue of her good name, but it had also denied her very existence. It had also sought to identify her tormentor, but it was looking increasingly likely that they had found the wrong guy and exposed him to potential violence.

The world responded to Amanda's suicide in ways that nobody could have predicted. While the response to a young girl taking her own life included sympathy and kindness, it also included calls for vengeance, hucksters trying to make a quick buck, self-appointed comedians who tried to make fun of it and morbid curiosity seekers trying to get more from her.

While Amanda had made no secret about wanting to become famous, there's no way she would have wanted any of that.

Chapter 10: Vengeance

While much of the online world was calling for Kody Maxson's head on a pike, the direction of the unsolicited, unprofessional investigation into the events leading up to Amanda Todd's suicide changed rapidly.

In fact, the day after NJAnon posted the YouTube video that claimed in no uncertain terms that her tormentor was Maxson, it posted another that said he wasn't. Although the language in the second video was much less direct, it shifted the blame from Maxson to Viper, the account Maxson himself had named when he spoke with the CTV reporter. In fact, several mainstream media sources in Britain and the rest of Europe cheerfully reported as a fact that Amanda's tormenter was American, even though he had not been identified as such by anyone but Maxson.

The Daily Capper awards video that mentioned both Kody1206 and Amanda briefly mentioned an account named Viper2323. He was nominated for their "most annoying" award. And the Daily Capper even got swept up in the newfound interest in the shadowy figure known as Viper, but was careful to implicate Maxson as, at least, a willing accomplice:

> "Viper and Kody worked alongside each other in groups, they trawled rooms together and even shared videos with each other. They continued working with each other till mid-2011. Kody was directly involved with Amanda in December, while he and Viper were still friends who shared videos with each other. Even if what Kody said were true, that would mean he knew Viper was blackmailing her the whole time and he did nothing to stop him because they shared videos with each other for long after. If Viper is the culprit, Kody was likely still involved and assisting him. That's assuming what Kody says is true."

Later, NJAnon tracked down a man they claimed was Viper2323. He was not from New York as Maxson had told CTV, but from Sheboygan, Wisconsin. They identified him as Danny Quach, a balding and married 41-year-old who, they said, along with his wife, "trolled dating sites looking for threesomes" before he started capping.

They revealed what they said were his memberships on several sites, including two notorious for sharing images of underage girls. It also linked to a Daily Capper video that says:

> "Viper and Kody worked alongside each other in groups, they trawled rooms together and even shared videos with each other. They continued working with each other till mid-2011. "Kody was directly involved with Amanda in December while he and Viper were still friends who shared videos with each other. Even if what Kody said were true, that would mean he knew Viper was blackmailing her the whole time and he did nothing to stop him because they shared videos with each other for long after. If Viper is the culprit, Kody was likely still involved and assisting him. That's assuming what Kody says is true."

But they stick to the idea of Maxson as the culprit in the Todd case, saying "while Viper may have been a pedophile, a troll, a psycho and many other things, one thing Viper was not was a blackmailer."

To back that up, they produced what they claimed was the transcript of an online conversation between Viper and another capper in which Viper refuses to deal with another capper because he blackmails girls.

The video ends with another denouncement of Maxson:

"Even if you wanted to believe his claims, you can be sure it all happened within his circle ... a small group of hackers and blackmailers, most of whom are infamous for using the exact same tactics used against Amanda. There's no big mystery here. Kody had been ID'd as a blackmailer even before it was a hot topic. If Kody was a hero ... why is there so much wrong with the logic of his story? Why were so many people able to connect him to Amanda as soon as she was being blackmailed?"

NJAnon and the Daily Capper seemed intent on naming Maxson as the tormentor, and Maxson blamed Viper. But while both men appeared to have been doing plenty that should have aroused the interest of law enforcement, nobody had provided any hard evidence that either was actually Todd's tormentor. Instead, it looked like the capper community was taking advantage of the media hype surrounding the Todd case to settle some old scores.

***

At about the same time, another video in reference to capping was posted to YouTube, by an account named Averyooo. In what journalist Kevin Morris described as a "Canadian accent," the narrator detailed how he became a capper.

After downloading some free video capture software, he began by capturing video from LiveJasmin — an immensely popular live video-chat site that employs adult models to communicate with paying customers — and sharing it with his friends. Before long, he said that he learned of other sites, on which girls (some of them underage) chatted and even stripped for free. By visiting those sites and capturing and trading the images, he said, he became a mainstay of the capper community.

The YouTube video and the account associated with it were quickly deleted.

***

Little information came from Canadian law enforcement when it came to the investigation of Todd's death. They had publicly written off Maxson, had made no mention of Quach and made no moves against individual bullies or the girls who had allegedly assaulted her.

In fact, public opinion of the local RCMP's efforts took a turn for the worse when a CBC report showed that Cybertip.ca, an organization dedicated to helping kids who are being bullied online, had received a concerned phone call about Amanda, warning that she could be in trouble, more than a year before her death. "We did receive one report, and that was passed along to law enforcement as well as child welfare," said Cybertip.ca spokeswoman Signy Arnason. "It was not a report from her, but it was a report from a concerned citizen." It quickly became apparent that Canadian law enforcement had not acted upon the tip.

While police in Canada appeared to be unable to prevent illegal images from being posted to Facebook pages regarding Amanda, that was not always the case in the rest of the world. On October 18, 2012, a 17-year-old boy in Raglan, New Zealand, received a visit from police.

According to their statement, police said the boy had posted "inappropriate and disturbing" images on a Facebook page dedicated to Todd's memory. Todd-watchers have told me that the images included the well-known flash picture in its original, unedited form as well as several "joke" pictures about her drinking bleach.

The Online Police Child Exploitation Across New Zealand (OCEANZ), a division of New Zealand's national police force, announced that it had received "more than 20 complaints" about the images from New Zealand and abroad.

While their meeting with the boy did not result in an arrest, the police did mete out some summary justice with the co-operation of his parents, according to the Waikato Times: "Police have removed the images and shut down his Facebook profile as well as taking other preventative steps to minimize further reproduction of these images."

***

While Anonymous had done its best to implicate Maxson (and he Quach), on the same day, another shocking video came to light that put the attention of the revenge-minded back on Maxson.

On the same BlogTV channel that Todd was alleged to have flashed on, another girl of about the same age posted a tell-all video claiming to have been victimized in much the same way Todd had been, and named Kody Maxson as the culprit.

Posted to YouTube by the Daily Capper, the girl, identified only as Peyton, identifies Maxson by his name, his real address and phone number and even the names of some of his family members (The Daily Capper muted those details for its post). It broadcast (in part):

Narrator: Peyton claims she is free of her blackmailers' clutches. She went on BlogTV to share her story of how Kody blackmailed her. She even got her mom to cuss him out …

Peyton: A month ago he recorded me for the first time, and then I was stupid enough to keep doing it because he said he'd never do it again, and he was stupid and he didn't want to ruin our relationship. And he just used me and he stopped calling me, stopped calling me and just wanted me out of his life because I gave him what he wanted. I have his address … he lives in Canada, I know his cousins' names, his family … his full name is Dakota William Shain Maxson … I know his phone number … I was just, like, liking the attention he was giving me. … Mom, cuss Kody out for me, he just [unintelligible] my email.

Narrator: Peyton admits she still wants to be with Kody.

But whether or not Peyton, if she was 15 as she claimed (and appeared), wanted to be with Kody or not, if he recorded her nude, he was breaking the law, and if he was extorting her for nudity, he was also breaking another law. But he was never charged with either offense.

Still, the Daily Capper claimed in its YouTube video that: "Many have been saying that Viper has always been a role model for Peyton's blackmailer, Kody1206. It seems Kody was also working to win Blackmailer of the Year by screening caps of Peyton on BlogTV."

But another Daily Capper video came out pointing out that Viper was also in a video discussion with Peyton when he revealed his actual age. "Seriously? And you watch … you wanna see a 14-year-old girl 'bate?" She then tells him her dad is a police officer and that he's already arrested three "pedos" in connection with her broadcasts.

On the same day, an account named WE ARE ANONYMOUS posted a video called "Anonymous - Amanda Todd [Kody Maxson]" to YouTube in which the now-familiar image of a person wearing a Guy Fawkes mask claimed that they knew who Amanda's bullies were, but offered no specific threats, just a request that they "take responsibility for what they did." It did, however, issue vague threats to those "who posted derogatory comments" on her video, although they acknowledged that they had not identified any of them. Despite the video's title, no other reference to Maxson is made.

***

On the same night, October 19, 2012, that those videos were released, a group called Global Girl Power organized a candlelight vigil in Amanda's honor in Holland Park in Surrey, B.C., not far from where she lived. Hundreds attended, and similar events were held, according to Global Girl Power, around the globe.

Surrey Mayor Dianne Watts spoke about the incident at the vigil:

> "Amanda's death has sparked outrage, grief — and to those who are still suffering in silence, I want to send one message: that there is help available and you are not alone. No child should feel such pain, loneliness and helplessness. Amanda's death has sparked outrage, grief and the collective coming together of all of us today to create change."

The Todds did not attend, but Surrey RCMP Superintendent Bill Fordy read a statement from them that said:

> "We are overwhelmed with your thoughts, prayers and love from each and every one of you. We would like to see changes made around the world to put an end to bullying once and for all."

About a week later, Carol Todd decided to speak to the media again. In an interview with the Vancouver Sun, which was broadcast on television in part by its partner Global TV, Carol added some detail to Amanda's last days. After leaving a hospital where she sought treatment for depression, Amanda told her mother that the same group of kids who had bullied her before had started calling her "psycho" and joking about how she had been in the "crazy house." Despite the torment that must have stood in the way of her attempts at recovery, Amanda told her mother that she was interested in starting to sing again, and perhaps rejoining the cheerleading team.

Carol pointed out that Amanda had always been a busy girl, and that she wasn't spending all her time on her computer, as many people on social media had claimed.

She also took the opportunity to defend herself from the legion of critics, almost all of whom hid behind pseudonyms, who put the blame for Amanda's death on her parenting skills and efforts. She said:

> "Was I the bad parent? No. Because at the ... the people who surround me will easily vouch for that. I did all I could for her."

Global TV posted a video of the interview on YouTube. Although many of the hundreds of comments it received have been deleted, virtually all of those that remain are examples of trolling, with frequent references to sex, scatological behavior, racism and criticism of people with developmental disorders. While those sorts of comments are not uncommon on YouTube, anything even remotely linked to Amanda Todd seems to attract an outrageous number of them.

Two weeks later, on October 11, 2012, another Amanda Todd-related video was posted to YouTube. An account named TheOfficialClown (its owner identifies himself as both Devyn Morris and Devyn DiAngelo) put up a video called "Amanda Todd's Final Video (4 Hours Before Death) Unseen RARE Footage."

With no sound other than a very sad acoustic version of Tears for Fears' Mad World by Gary Jules, it's one of the Mandaa&Shyy videos, clearly recorded much earlier than its owner claimed. It appears that TheOfficialClown had fudged the facts on the title to get a high number of views. It worked. Although revealing nothing, the video has received in excess of 650,000 views (which translates to about $900 to $2,200, depending on who's viewing) and, as I write this, 2,146 comments.

Of those comments that are not requests for the name of the song being played, most are by trolls blaming Amanda for her own fate or making jokes about drinking bleach. The bulk of the remainder are replies in defense of Amanda.

***

Cooper Fleishman, who had been at the forefront of revealing leaked information about the case, published an article on November 7, 2012 that dug deeper into the allegations Peyton had made to the Daily Capper and the capper world in general. In it, he found that Peyton was linked not just to Kody1206 and Viper2323, but another alleged capper who went by the names R0, r044, r0r044 or rora-anon.

He pointed to a page on anon-pass.org, a proxy server that allows users to visit any website without their IP number or any other identifying data showing up. Posted on September 29, 2011 (more than a year before Amanda's death), was an article called "Rora anon has been doxed, Internet troll/pedophile." It begins with a screen cap of a tidy-looking young man — perhaps in his twenties — with a short haircut. He's holding up a sign that reads:

"POST NO WIN (=
R0 <3 PEY 9/24"

The sign has been interpreted to mean either that rora-anon is asking Peyton not to take her clothes off on camera because he loves her or that he won't share any of the nude caps he has of her for the same reason.

It's followed by a description of rora-anon that accuses him of trolling "newfags" (inexperienced cappers) by promising them win and providing links, but not giving them the necessary passwords to access them.

Shockingly, it then accuses him of capping a 12-year-old girl who later committed suicide. And it goes on to say that "some anon's on anonib and other chan's think he is a murderer as well" because of his involvement with the suicide. Anonib is a website that allowed users to post images anonymously, and the "chan's" mentioned refer to the many sites that emerged and copied 4chan's style after its success.

The post continues to accuse rora-anon of illegal behavior, claiming that "R0r44 is known for having recordings of girls so young they could very well be boys and you wouldn't tell if it wasn't for the explicitness of his recordings."

But the post claims that rora-anon slipped up and lost his anonymity when he fell in love with Peyton, who they say leaked caps of his face on Anonib. It also says that there are also pictures of rora-anon cutting himself so that he could write a love letter to Peyton in his own blood, but for reasons of good taste, the author refused to post them.

There are 18 comments on the post, and all of them except for one appear to be generic attempts to drive traffic to other blogs with complimentary notes (like "nice blog post") and links to ad sites that have no relation to the article. The other, from a since-discontinued account simply named Alex, asks "Who is that 12yo girl that killed herself? Sophh from timgreek? Or any other?" It was posted March 10, 2012, seven months before Amanda's death.

While there is no direct connection between Amanda Todd and rora-anon given in the article, it does link him to both Kody1206 and Peyton. It also gives some details of the capper community and his role in it, and claims that at least one other young girl was known by them to have committed suicide because of the cappers' actions. In fact, the comment from Alex makes it seem as though several girls might have met that very fate.

***

The anti-bullying machine that had been given so much extra fuel by the amount of coverage Amanda's suicide had received kept chugging along.

November 12 was the start of National Anti-Bullying Month in Canada. The theme, its organizers said was "stand up" — which they explained "encourages Canadians of all ages to acknowledge that bullying exists, but it's also important to strive for change." It was the kind of endearingly vague message that made people feel good about themselves without any actual specific call to action.

Kids Help Phone, a counselling service that had been around since 1989, did its part by producing a 30-second video in which several well-known but not exactly top echelon Canadian pop entertainers — Jacob Hoggard, Lights, Pierre Bouvier, Fefe Dobson, Kardinal Offishall, Alyssa Reid and Walk Off the Earth — sang a version of Cyndi Lauper's minor 1986 hit True Colors, with the lyrics changed to reflect an anti-bullying stance. In what appears to be an homage to Amanda's own video, the artists dropped placards with pertinent words on them, and it was shot in black and white.

Proceeds from iTunes sales of the song and video went to Kids Help Phone.

Chapter 11: War of Words

As the war of videos between Anonymous and The Daily Capper waged on YouTube, Vice.com journalist Patrick McGuire pointed out in an article that neither side had earned anything close to resembling credibility and that they were far from trustworthy. He also noted that despite their "moralizing tones," both sides appeared to have been sitting on important evidence like videos, still photos, chat logs, emails and other important evidence that they published well after Amanda's death (and up to two years after their creation) rather than sharing them with law enforcement. And since they had meted out just snippets of heavily edited evidence, he surmised that they were surely in possession of much more potentially enlightening evidence.

And that, although both sides were more than happy to name Kody Maxson as the culprit, they could produce nothing more than weak circumstantial evidence supporting their claim, and the actual authorities had said that they had investigated him and found him to be a "person of no interest" in the case.

So McGuire did his own investigation of both Maxson and NJAnon. He determined that NJAnon, which claimed to be a Northern New Jersey "branch" of a greater Anonymous organization, was founded after Amanda's suicide and seemed to be dedicated to it and it alone as it had posted about nothing else on YouTube and Twitter. When he asked them why they had taken up the cause, they answered:

> "I'm pretty certain that Kody was involved with Amanda's death. He's a known pedophile with charges against him. He has blackmailed other girls over webcam in the same manner and he has admitted to being friends with her online. I know it's not hard evidence, but he looks guilty to me."

Later, McGuire and an IT security expert who was willing to help but not have his name published established an email address called kody.maxson@hotmail.com (they were surprised it was available, but agreed it could well have been previously used and then abandoned). Without any solicitation, it rapidly filled with death threats and media inquiries. That indicated that the campaigns by the Daily Capper and NJAnon to link Maxson to Amanda's death, or even blame him for it, were working with at least some part of the public.

To find out more about Maxson, McGuire then Googled his name, but to get through the thousands of recent articles and posts that linked him to Amanda, he simply filtered out any responses that also mentioned her. One of the first items to return was a link to a Facebook post in reference to the 2011 Vancouver riots that raged after the Canucks lost the Stanley Cup. It was "liked" by a Facebook account named Kody Maxson, which also commented "fun night."

Following the link to the Kody Maxson account, McGuire found that its name had been changed to John Doee, but that it's URL was facebook.com/kody604 (Vancouver's primary area code is 604). Although the account gave a Havana, Cuba, home address, the rest of it jibed with what the media already knew about Maxson. Although he also claimed to have attended Hogwarts, the account's holder also admitted to having gone to Semiahoo Secondary School and Earl Marriott Secondary School in Surrey, both of which Maxson is known to have attended.

The search also led McGuire to Websites R' Us, a website-design firm that claimed to be based in Delta, B.C. It was loaded with spelling and grammatical errors, and looked unlikely to have successfully drummed up any business, but it did reveal a few clues. Its contact email was kody.maxson@hotmail.com (the same one McGuire had previously set up to gauge public opinion of Maxson), and the site's URL was kody1206.wix.com. Of course, the Kody1206 handle had appeared all over the internet, often in association with video-streaming, capping and jailbait sites and forums.

Of course, Kody1206 was a big part of the next Daily Capper awards show. The narrator describes the Blackmailer of the Year award as the most prestigious the organization has to offer and refers to the nominees as "rapists." Despite facing stiff challenges from Perso — who is described as "enjoying time with sex slaves while they drink out of the toilet" — and Aussie — who is said to have "blackmailed so many times, he does not know if he's doing it or not" — Kody1206 won. The narrator commended him, noting he was "famous for his blackmail of Peyton, streaming her videos on BlogTV and TinyChat, and threatening her in public."

It seems as though both The Daily Capper and NJAnon were working hard to make a scapegoat out of Maxson through hype rather than due process. Their attempts to rile up a modern-day lynch mob — which had actually resulted in nothing more than a plethora of empty, anonymous death threats — was clearly failing.

Plenty of people were convinced that Maxson was guilty simply because they wanted an identifiable villain. That mindset is not rare. There's an old saying in Mexico that if a crime is committed, somebody goes to jail. It might not be the guy who committed that crime, but he probably deserved it anyway.

Of course, Maxson did very little to help his own case. On November 29, 2012, two days after what would have been Amanda's 16th birthday, it was widely reported that he skipped a court date to answer charges of theft under $5,000, sexual assault and sexual interference with a minor, and a warrant was issued for his arrest.

It was, to many people, a cut-and-dried case: Maxson was linked to Amanda, he was accused of capping and threatening her by both the Daily Capper and NJAnon, and he also appeared to be on the run from the law after refusing to face charges that allegedly included sexual assault on a minor.

But thought leaders refused to give into that mentality. And those in law enforcement wre not allowed to.

Of course, even a cursory inspection of the sources would lead anyone to question the accusers' ethics, credibility and motivation.

The Daily Capper is, by their own admission, a group whose defining reason for existence is to capture pictures and videos of girls nude, including underage ones, and to use those images to extort them for more. To think that they would want to punish Maxson for doing exactly that would be absurd. Hadn't they just given him their top award for his efforts? But if they were naming him publicly in relation to Amanda, it was to indict him, not to praise him.

Did their new-found morality arise because Amanda was just 15? Hardly. Much of what they had made public in previous videos had reflected a preference for underage girls as victims. Because she had killed herself? Doubtful. They did not show a lot of compassion for the girls who were compelled to drink out of toilets.

It's far more likely that Maxson was ordered to walk the plank because he had done something else to anger another capper or group of cappers. It's important to keep in mind that all of the information provided by The Daily Capper was identical to the original claims by kodypwned, who also admitted to being a capper and even admitted that he threatened to extort Amanda to get Maxson's email address.

And NJAnon, who took pride in describing themselves as "cruel" rather than just or fair, seemed somehow even less credible than a group of people dedicated to the sexual extortion of children. They appeared to be genuinely confused about the case, frequently contradicting themselves, and changing their collective mind about what they had held firmly as fact just days earlier. They admitted they could well be wrong about Maxson, but also said they didn't care, just that he deserved to be punished.

Again, their efforts seemed less like a group looking for justice for Amanda than a bunch of people with a grudge against Maxson in particular.

Just as there were people interested in the case who accepted the word of anyone calling themselves Anonymous without much thought, more and more came to the opinion that the credibility of anyone who refuses to make their name and credentials public isn't really worth the bandwidth it takes up.

It was at about that time that the media covering the event had clearly divided into three distinct groups.

First there was the mainstream media, which seemed content to leave all investigation to law enforcement and instead concentrate on how concerts, ribbons and bracelets were going to eradicate bullying in our time. To them, the primary culprits were the kids in the schoolyard; the ones who called Amanda retard, camwhore and psycho. But they stopped well short of calling for any specific action against any individuals.

That point of view was made evident when Canadian Senator Mobina Jaffer appeared on BBC World Service radio to speak about the tragedy and investigation. McGuire managed to call in and ask her why the government was investigating the bullying Amanda received from her peers and not the extortion demands she had received online, pointing out that one was easily identifiable and actionable as a crime and the other wasn't. "Of course the predator is a very big issue," she said. "But where we have been focusing is the issue of friends, cyber-bullying continuing from the school ground to the Facebook, to the Twitter, to the internet."

That opinion was countered by the serious online journalists like Fleishman and McGuire who were reporting everything they could about how and why Amanda was capped and blackmailed — and who was actually involved. Although they diligently reported all the evidence they could find, they were largely limited to the announcements made by two less-than-credible sources in The Daily Capper and Anonymous. To this second group, the responsible parties were those who capped and extorted Amanda, even if they could not or would not actually determine who they were.

And there emerged a third group online. Led by a man who claimed to have been a former mainstream reporter and went by the name Philip J. Rose online because his writing on the subject had earned him death threats, they reported much of the same material as the other two groups, but took an entirely different spin on the story. Their thesis was that Amanda had brought torment upon herself by what they considered to be her wanton online behavior and backed it up by reporting how frequently she had appeared online either nude or scantily dressed, even after she had been threatened.

Rose, in particular, called out Amanda's parents as responsible, claiming that they had allowed her to remain online unsupervised even after they were aware that she had received the blackmailer's demands. He frequently referred to Carol Todd as an "idiot" and threatened to "slap" her if he saw her in person, and obliquely appeared to accuse Norm Todd of being a willing participant of Amanda's online activities.

Chapter 12: 'Princess Snowflake'

While people in government, media and social media were competing to be heard, the Todd family and their allies continued to grieve. A memorial was held at the Red Robinson Show Theater in Coquitlam on November 16, 2012. Pointing out that Amanda always hoped that her neighbors Christmas lights would be up before her November 27 birthday, Carol Todd said that every house on their cul-de-sac had Christmas lights up and on already. "Amanda, you will be happy to know this year, most of the neighbourhood friends — I think all of them now — have already put up their lights in honour of you," she said, reading aloud a letter she wrote to her daughter.

She then went on to explain that her nickname for Amanda had been "Princess Snowflake," in part because of her fondness for snow and winter sports. "Three weeks ago, I looked up the definitions to the word snowflake," Carol told those in attendance. "Most were pretty standard meanings, then in the Urban Dictionary online I found this: 'Snowflake: A very unique girl that no one else can duplicate because she is one of a kind.' That was you my Princess

Snowflake — you were indeed a unique individual who I don't think can ever be duplicated. You have been an amazing daughter, a sister and a friend." It's odd that she would go to Urban Dictionary, which is dedicated to defining some of the most appallingly graphic slang.

There were other speakers, including Pells, Amanda's teacher from C.A.B.E. "Her tenderness was always with her, no matter what things were going on in her life; the individuals she touched will always be better for having loved her," she said. "She was surrounded in love but it was not enough for what she was dealing with."

There were other tributes, and local musicians Cole Armour, Michaela Slinger and Elise Estrada sang tributes. Nobody spoke of the extortionist, and bullying was mentioned only obliquely. In fact, the only actual mention of bullying at the tribute (and one of the few things anybody had said in the whole tragedy that indicated action) came from Amanda herself. In a letter she had written that was read at the tribute, she wrote: "I hope that someday I can write a song about bullying so when kids are alone staring out their windows crying, they can listen to my song and know that it's not your fault and things will get better."

***

At about that time, an online user posted a question on Yahoo Answers under the title Why are people still bullying Amanda Todd? It read:

> Amanda was my best friend. She was always there for me and i was always there for her. We were more like sisters than best friends. Everything got out of hand. Now that ive lost my best friend as hard as it is there are still people bullying her. People telling her to go die with bleach, did it taste nice, and people are having a party to celebrate that she has left us. She never deserved any of this. She was the nicest girl i ever knew. She

will always ve my best friend no matter!!!! R.I.P Amanda!! love
you forever!

Many of the answers called the poster out for not doing enough
to prevent Amanda's suicide or simply to show disdain for Amanda
herself. One, who went by the name James, wrote: "your best friend
was an attention whore and some people don't fall for her tricks.
Simple as that." Another, Mike, wrote: "wasent she a hoe?...she
****** a guy that she wasent even dating sluuuuuuu...and she kept
showing her tists everywhere im sorry but to me she just sounds like
a stupid hoe lol"

Chapter 13: Media Coverage

The first thing you notice about Norman Todd is how much he and his daughter look alike. Of course, he's a middle-aged man and she was just a kid and she never had his piercing blue eyes, but the resemblance is otherwise astounding. If Amanda had not become a household name by then, you probably would have said she looked like him.

On November 15, 2012, the public got their first really close look at Norm Todd when he gave a video interview to CTV News.

Seated on a couch that was draped with a Vancouver Canucks blanket and holding Amanda's little terrier, Charlee, he spoke directly to the camera. Almost as soon as the interview begins, he understandably starts to tear up.

He describes life with his daughter as idyllic before the torment began. "When things were going good in her life, the good times we had together, she was just a blast," Todd said. "High-spirited, wanted to do everything, wanted to explore, try everything ... I miss that terribly."

That was a typical description of Amanda's life before the extortionist struck. She was just a regular kid with many of the same ups and downs other kids face, but with a positive attitude.

He also spoke about how after the problems began, he and Amanda had promised to get matching tattoos on their arms. The tattoos would say "stay strong" and have a little red heart. It was, he said, her idea and was intended to remind her that she had to stay strong, not give up and use her courage to get through her problems.

After her death, he did get the tattoo. The event was covered by CTV News at Port Coquitlam's Ink 'n' Honey Tattoo Shop, and the ink, they said, had some of Amanda's ashes mixed in.

When asked about the original tormentor, he called out the police. "I want to see nothing more than this pedophile caught," he said. "It makes me mad, it makes me hurt. I would love to see this person brought to justice."

Norm didn't appear to have a high opinion of the police efforts, though. He told the reporter about how he had gone to them after his daughter had been assaulted by the other girls at school. He had disappointed that they had refused to act at the time, preferring to leave the issue to schoolyard justice. "I don't think they chased it hard enough at that time. I don't think it was taken seriously enough," he said. "I think they should've done something about those girls. People are ruthless. They just kept attacking her for whatever reason, they thought it was fun."

The reporter pointed out that the RCMP had put together an investigative team of 20 to 25 investigators after Amanda's death.

While Norman Todd broke his silence with a one-and-done CTV News interview, Carol Todd seemed to be everywhere in the media. While she spoke primarily with The Vancouver Sun, Carol frequently could be found on TV, at fundraising and bullying awareness events and online. She blogged not only on her own site — Carol Todd's Snowflakes — but also on Huffington Post and Dr. Phil's site and was photographed rubbing elbows with more than a few big-time celebrities. Some on social media accused her of pursuing her own fame.

In fact, there was something of a media stir in November 2012 when Carol found out that the B.C. government was holding an anti-bullying conference — the Erase Bullying Summit — and she was not invited. After finding out that she could not invite herself (the province said her presence might upset some of the students at the conference, even though four other sets of parents whose children had committed suicide were invited to attend), Carol called The Vancouver Sun. They ran an article about it, pointing out that Carol didn't even want to speak at the conference, just to attend. Carol then went to Twitter, posting: "It is a shame that I was excluded from the forum .. is that form of bullying?"

The province answered her through another media source, 1130 News radio. A spokesman for the Ministry of Education, which was holding the conference, said that Carol would be allowed to send a representative and that Education Minister Don McRae would meet with her personally to discuss the issues brought up at the summit.

Carol was further angered when she learned that Real Housewives of Vancouver cast member Mary Zilba was invited to speak as an expert. Things got even more muddied when B.C. Premier Christy Clark said that it wasn't her "understanding" that Carol had been excluded and then said to a group of reporters: "We lost Amanda and it was a tragedy but we should learn from that. She would want that from us."

Carol responded on her blog, saying: "Yes, Amanda would have wanted us to learn from her message and I am the one who knows best what Amanda would have wanted us to do and that would be to use her message to help others and to have her mother there in the process. Both her father and I are stunned by the process of events and even more so as an educator in our province." She also said that she thought that Clark and others were benefitting from the public grief over Amanda's death, citing the fact that the premier had appeared in a condolence video on YouTube without notifying her first.

It appeared as though Carol wanted a say in any media or political version of the Amanda Todd story.

***

But while the police had declared Maxson a "person of no interest," lots of other people had not given up on the idea that he was guilty and should be punished. One of them was an activist YouTuber who went by the name of EnigmaHood. He had made a number of strident videos, and he called for the incarceration, at the very least, of Maxson. And it was he who would be the first to talk to him once the police had absolved him.

That is, if it was really him.

The nature of their discussion — and much of what this book is about — is clouded by the anonymity of internet identities. What we do know is that someone who calls himself EnigmaHood received a call from someone named Gei who claimed to be the ex-girlfriend of Kody Maxson. And she set up a Skype video call so that EnigmaHood could interview Maxson.

EnigmaHood recorded the conversation, and sent it to Vice.com reporter Patrick McGuire, who had already exposed much of what the world actually knew about Maxson and the other cappers caught up in the Todd story.

The call went to a Skype account with no picture and the name r4p3-k0dy. For those who are familiar with l33t, it was an eyebrow-raising choice. For those who aren't, l33t or l33tsp34k is a sort-of code used by people who consider themselves to be hackers or at least better-than-average computer users. There are many variations, but most l33t users simply replace vowels with numbers that look like them. For example, 3s look like Es, so l33t means leet (and l33tspe4k means leetspeak) a derivation of the self-congratulatory title "elite." So r4p3-k0dy actually means rape-kody.

The account gave Vancouver as its location, although the caller later said he was in Cuba.

McGuire determined that there was only one r4p3-k0dy online after a deep internet search. He had also found a YouTube video by someone who called herself Gei called Rant on Pointless Suicide (that was uploaded a few days after Amanda's death) in which she criticized people who make anti-bullying videos for wasting their and her time and for being insincere.

One of the comments it received was from a user named bountyhunter176. It said: "Gei add my skype you know who it is, r4p3-kody."

That led McGuire to find a conversation between Gei and r4p3-kody on PasteBin. It's long and arduous to read due to poor grammar and spelling, so I have summarized the essential details:

- Gei mentions that she is 14 years old, (if r4p3-kody is Maxson, he's at least 19 at the time of the chat), and asks for help getting a new account on an adult online chat site that turfed her after finding out that she was underage
- He coerces her to give him her password to show "mutual respect and trust." Despite her initial resistance, in which she says: "Nah, fuck that. You've fucked me over before... You limit me to what I can and cannot do... You try to control me... I fucking hate that," then she relents and says "Fucking happy?"
- He indicates that he's jealous that she's playing the mega-popular Minecraft online with other guys, and asks for access to her game, saying "If u dont gimme the link im never guna talk to you again... Theirs 2 ways this can go. You gimme the link im nice etc. 2nd way when i do figure it out ill hack it;" she refuses, saying "Kody, no. You screen shot everything. And use it against me later"
- He gets sexual, asking her if she likes it "rough kinky or passionate" and says he want to "dominate the fuck outta" her.

In the rambling interview, EnigmaHood badgers r4p3-kody, and tells his audience that Gei told him that she also thinks Kody is guilty and that he should "go to prison where he belongs."

But to his credit, EnigmaHood did ask r4p3-k0dy to provide his side of the story. Surprisingly, r4p3-k0dy refused. He said he didn't really want to get into it, and that he was just "pissed off" about what he had seen about himself in the media, and was upset that people believed it. He admitted that he knew Amanda "for a little bit" as a friend, but was never in any possession of her flashing pictures and denied even wanting to see them.

EngimaHood then asks why, if he's innocent, NJAnon named him as the culprit. He replied that "I pissed them off because of the shit I was doing to them through certain hacking groups online."

McGuire told NJAnon what r4p3-k0dy had said, and they responded by telling him: "I really doubt he can hack, and I would say that I didn't know who he even was before that day in October when I researched him. So, his claim that we are attacking him because he made us mad is unfounded."

But EnigmaHood can't contain his rage in the interview, and calls r4p3-k0dy a "piece of shit." At that, r4p3-k0dy leaves the call. Gei stays on and tells EnigmaHood that she has "doubts in her head" about Kody's involvement with Amanda, but then says she needs no proof of Kody's innocence other than his word.

***

And while millions were watching Amanda's video, not everyone was comfortable allowing their kids see it.

In the days when Amanda was still front-page news in Canada, a teacher at Goodwood Public School in Uxbridge, Ontario, decided to show Amanda's video to her Grade 5 and 6 class.

That day, an area father, Paul Kreutzer, was saddened to see his 10-year-old daughter come home in tears. In fact, she had left school early, telling the administrators that she was sick and had to leave. When her father asked her why, she told him that the teacher had shown her class the video, and that she was so disturbed that she could not carry on her school day.

Concerned, Kreutzer then watched the video and objected to the teacher showing his child media that included topics "of a sexual nature."

He complained, calling the teacher's action "reckless" and "highly inappropriate" and pointing out that other parents were just as angry as he was. The school declined to comment for the media, but Kreuzter said that: "The teacher in question, I guess, has a history of being a social worker." And he found out that it wasn't the first time the same teacher had exposed his daughter to information he found offensive. "For some reason or another she started sharing information about specific case details," he said. "A case she worked as a social worker where the father came home and murdered the kids."

The teacher was not disciplined, but Durham Region school superintendent said that showing the Todd video in class was "clearly not acceptable."

Interestingly, most mainstream media outlets that carried the story did not name the teacher, the school or even the town.

Chapter 14: Fighting Bullying

The Amanda Todd story seemed like it wouldn't leave, that it could not be stopped. Carol Todd wanted to control it, the mainstream media wanted to focus of bullying (including at least two think pieces on how bullying is the root cause for suicide bombers), the online media wanted to catch the culprit before the police did and millions of people just wanted to praise or condemn the girl online.

Yahoo revealed that Amanda Todd was the world's sixth-most searched subject of 2012, right behind princess-to-be Kate Middleton, even though the story of her suicide only broke in October. Similarly, Google announced that Amanda's was the fourth-most searched-for death in 2012.

A survey of 24,000 kids conducted by Safer Internet Day, a U.K.-based anti-bullying charity, indicated that their No. 1 fear was online bullying. But it should be noted that the survey was done a month after Amanda's suicide.

Everybody seemed to want to get in on the act.

Three students at a Port Coquitlam high school Amanda had not attended founded a set of Twitter and Facebook accounts dedicated to helping bullied kids by sending random compliments to them. Although hundreds of kids signed up, it's hard to see how no-specific, one-size-fits-all complimentary messages in your inbox would help if you were being extorted and assaulted. And it also identified the targets of bullying, exposing them to reprisals.

At about the same time, a 14-year-old high school student from Coxheath, Nova Scotia, named Callum Pickles developed an anti-bullying app called Your Privacy. The app scans the user's social media feed for bullying language (he suggested the word "loser") and points it out to the user, asking them whether they want it deleted and reported to the social media company's administrators.

Pickles said he was moved by Amanda's plight, but also said he had not seen bullying in his own school (despite Cape Breton Island's rough-and-tumble reputation):

> "The Amanda Todd case, that's one of the reason that really got me up to do this. There's been so many suicides from cyberbullying. Nobody really has the guts to face them in person. When they are in a pack with a bunch of friends they might pick on them, but if they are face-to-face they won't. Online, they just want to be hidden and will act so tough when they are behind a computer."

Calls for anti-bullying laws increased. Although civil liberties advocates pointed out that Canada had lots of laws that would have helped Amanda had they actually been enforced and that even to begin to curtail free speech was a dangerous road to take, the calls kept getting louder.

And they took hold in Hanna, a small agricultural town in Alberta's Short Grass Country. In a town council meeting at which Amanda's suicide was discussed, the town passed a law under which bullying language could lead to a $250 fine and multiple offenses could lead to bigger fines and even jail.

But what's interesting is where the idea for the law came from. It wasn't a grassroots activist group of concerned parents or frightened teens; it was Canada's state-run police force. "The RCMP approached us — they didn't have a mechanism for dealing with bullying short of when it becomes a Criminal Code offence," said Hanna mayor Mark Nikota. "It's mainly to give the RCMP ... another mechanism to help in those situations."

Other Alberta communities adopted similar statutes. Airdrie, a suburb of Calgary, passed its own anti-bullying laws after councilors heard from a girl who said she had been through similar circumstances. Mackenzie Murphy moved to Airdrie after she had been bullied online. She hadn't flashed and wasn't being extorted, she just put herself up on Facebook and ran a blog of her thoughts. But when people started to comment on both — often with foul language, threats and entreaties to kill herself — her mother moved her to Airdrie, but the bullying started again.

In fact, Murphy — just 13 — was in an Airdrie hospital recovering from a suicide attempt when Hanna passed its anti-bullying law. Murphy's mother, Tara, told reporters that Carol Todd had been a great help to her.

So had the RCMP. Constable David Henry, who works with Airdrie schools, also lent support. "When I first started working in the schools about five years ago, about 15 percent of my job consisted of Facebook and texting bullying," he said. "Now I'm up to about 90 percent online bullying."

After the law passed, Murphy told reporters: "I think kids will be scared to bully after this — I've already had other kids asking me what they have to do to report people who do this."

But as well intentioned as the town might have been, they still had the same problems the RCMP had — defining exactly what language is actually actionable, finding out who the anonymous online bullies were and what to do about them if they weren't in their jurisdiction.

But that was just part a small of the cultural phenomenon that was unleashed by Amanda's video. As 2013 soldiered on, people held rallies and vigils, made videos and short films and called for change.

As the anti-bullying train was gaining steam, Canada was hit with another tragedy. Rehteah Parsons, a 17-year-old from Cole Harbour, Nova Scotia, committed suicide in April 2013 after being bullied. Pictures of her drunk and having sex —media referred to it as a "gang rape" — when she was just 15 were circulated around her high school.

At the time of the original event — the boys involved said the sex was consensual, although it appeared to many as though Parsons was too drunk to consent legally — the RCMP did not pursue charges. They told her parents that it was a "he said, she said" situation. Not long after, when a friend of Parsons' was stabbed, allegedly by one of the boys Parsons named in the incident after a verbal confrontation about her, the police again refused to lay charges, due to a lack of sufficient evidence.

After Parson died in April 7, 2013, her mother started a Facebook page called Angel Rehtaeh. It was an immediate sensation, and received comments and visit from all over the world in huge numbers. It was countered by Facebook pages and demonstrations condemning Parsons, calling her a "slut" and demanding "justice" for the boys.

Media attention followed, declaring bullying-caused suicide an epidemic. Prime Minister Stephen Harper commented, saying that what happened to Parsons and Todd was "sickening," but that it was the result of crimes already on the books, and that bullying was not a criminal act unless the bullies broken existing laws.

A day later, the RCMP re-opened the Parsons case, citing "new and credible information." They took great pains to point out that it did not come from the internet.

Again, people calling themselves Anonymous launched an investigation without being asked. But they declined to publish their findings, they said, out of respect for the Parsons family. The odd part of that was names of the boys alleged to have been involved were all over the internet, even though they were still minors.

Two of the boys were eventually convicted in 2014. One of them, then 20, was found guilty of making child pornography. He was given 12 months' probation and a conditional discharge, which meant no criminal record. The other, then 19, was guilty of making and distributing child pornography, which netted him a year of probation, but no discharge. He also had to submit DNA to a nationwide database.

But even as the Parsons case gave it new life, the public outrage over Amanda Todd's persecution and suicide began to fade. It's just how things happen. Because neither her extortionist nor her bullies had been conclusively named, there was no real villain other than the internet, and you can only shake your fist at it so long. Even the official Amanda Todd memorial page on Facebook began to change, putting up posts discussing boy bands and advertising used iPhones.

At least Todd's supporters could feel good about the fact that they had made a lot of people at least think about the consequences of bullying.

Chapter 15: An Arrest

I t was in January 2014 — at least a year after law enforcement seemed to have anything to say to the media about the Todd case — when I received a text from a friend who knew I was interested in the story. "They caught the guy who blackmailed Amanda Todd," it read.

Indeed, an arrest had been made. A man in the Netherlands — Aydin Coban (also spelled Çoban) — had been taken into custody facing charges related to online extortion. After a few days, he was connected in the media to Amanda Todd, among others. The RCMP laid charges against him in the Todd case on top of those he already faced in the Netherlands.

How they found him was as strange as everything else involved in the Todd story.

While police maintained for years that they had little to act on and Anonymous seemed to have moved onto other targets, individuals, mainly using Facebook, were still trying to find out everything they could about the identity of the alleged tormentor. They uncovered plenty of tenuous clues linking her to Coban — including evidence that someone who went by the initials AC had chatted with Todd online and that another girl reported being blackmailed by a person from the Netherlands in similar circumstances — but nothing that came close to identifying a single person.

That was, until Facebook's own security measures kicked in. The Menlo Park, California-based company has many sophisticated algorithms built into its security software that are specifically designed to target fictitious or predatory users. Among them are filters that automatically red flag accounts that send an improbably large proportion of their friend requests to female users or make frequent requests to alter their birth date information.

According to Coban's Amsterdam-based lawyer, Christian van Dijk, Facebook noticed that one IP address in particular had been setting up a large number of accounts — at least 20 — that were rapidly attracting friends, many of them young women and girls, at a very rapid pace.

Facebook prepared a report on the IP address (77.165.109.4), which they handed to the FBI, who shared it with the Child Exploitation and Online Protection Centre (which is part of the U.K. National Crime Agency) and other law enforcement organizations. It is not clear if the RCMP was among them, and Amanda Todd's name had not appeared in the original Facebook investigation.

After their own four-month investigation, the Dutch national police (Korps landelijke politiediensten or KLPD) had gathered enough evidence to arrest Coban at his cabin in Bungalowpark de Rosep, a small community made up mainly of Eastern European immigrants and guest workers who commute to the nearby city of Oisterwijk.

Normally, such an arrest would receive little notice in the media — they happen all the time — but the KLPD let it be known that a search of Coban's laptop revealed a Facebook account under the name Tyler Boo. After that, newspapers and websites all over the world reported that Amanda Todd's alleged blackmailer had been caught.

"I don't think the police made this case," said Coban's lawyer van Dijk. "I think Facebook made this case. They put it all together."

Facebook acknowledged its part in the investigation in a terse statement for the media: "In the rare instance when this illegal behavior is detected in our community, we have strict guidelines for working with law enforcement to bring suspected criminals to justice and keep Facebook a safe place."

Three months after the KLPD laid charges for nine offences, including indecent assault and production and dissemination of child pornography, the RCMP slapped Coban with five charges including extortion, internet luring, criminal harassment and the possession and distribution of child pornography — all directly related to his alleged interaction with Todd.

***

Coban, the Dutch-born son of Turkish immigrants, sits in a cell at Penitentiaire Inrichting Nieuwegein as I write this. Todd is hardly his only alleged victim. The Dutch originally charged him in relation to extortion attempts against as many as 75 victims in Denmark, the U.S., U.K. and Canada.

Along with attempts to extort nudity from girls, Dutch police allege that Coban was part of a large scheme in which a team of would-be extortionists would pose as underage boys online, then chat flirtatiously with men. When the men became overtly sexual, authorities maintain, the capper would then capture the comment or act and use it to extort money from the victim. The extortion of girls, they alleged, was a side hobby that employed the skills learned in his extortion business.

Coban certainly fits the public perception of the kind of person who would blackmail a child for his own sexual gratification.

He was a 35-year-old loner. Neighbors in Bungalowpark de Rosep told reporters they knew very little about him (his landlord initially denied to at least one reporter that Coban even lived there before eventually admitting that he did after she was shown police statements). He had no wife, girlfriend or kids, did not have any close friends at work, did not attend any nearby mosques and stayed indoors almost all the time. Pictures show him as a weak-chinned fellow with a unibrow and greasy, ill-kempt hair.

He maintains that he is innocent. Just as Maxson before him, Coban claims that he was the subject of an elaborate "hate campaign."

Coban wrote an open letter from jail that the Dutch authorities allowed media to publish in January 2015. Coban writes in a stilted but otherwise generally correct English (something Maxson would struggle to do, but that Tyler Boo usually did) because, he said, it in an international case.

"First off, I'm innocent," he wrote. "I'm not the so-called tormentor of Miss Amanda Todd or of anyone else, for that matter. I've been in jail exactly a year now for things I haven't done."

His letter then rails against the Dutch authorities. "They pretend to be the judge, the jury and the executioner while committing character assassination by orchestrating a hate campaign against an individual on a scale rarely seen."

Coban says that it's a case of mistaken identity. His letter makes the claim that he was using a neighbor's router for internet, and that it was actually the router's IP address, not his laptop's, that the threatening messages to Todd and others came from. He also writes that many in the community used the same router at the time of the alleged crimes.

From there, he accuses the Dutch investigators of using unnamed "secretive tools" in an effort to "infect" his laptop, and placing incriminating evidence on it. Their motive, he said, was to find a fall guy to put an end to the case, even though the blackmails had gone largely unreported and the Todd case had grown cold.

A few weeks after his arrest, Dutch authorities dropped the child pornography charges and charges related to victims outside of the Netherlands against Coban. The Dutch were not going to prosecute him in the Todd case. "We have no intention to do so, because it's a Canadian case, which has been investigated thoroughly in Canada for years," said prosecution spokesman Pal van der Zanden. "Not mentioning the fact that a suspect cannot be tried in two different countries for the same crime."

The province of British Columbia sent an extradition request to Ottawa to relay to Amsterdam so that Coban can face charges —

including those of child pornography — in relation to Todd in Canada after his trial in the Netherlands.

"Those charges still stand, and our B.C. Crown is still looking at extraditing him," Carol Todd told CTV News. "There is no talk that they will drop this, so I can only hope that that's what happens."

Despite the fact that Coban's team has asked for more time to gather evidence, his trial is set for April 29, 2016. His extradition hearing is scheduled for May 12.

***

If you look at the media coverage of Amanda Todd's death, you'll see lots of memorials, almost as many crude jokes and a huge number of anti-bullying messages.

And now, you'll see plenty of triumphant posts that claim her original tormenter has finally been caught. Of course, there are still a few out there who vehemently claim that the authorities have got the wrong guy. There's just something about this story that makes people think they're not getting the whole story or that they're being lied to.

What you won't see is anyone identifying or calling for the punishment of her schoolyard aggressors or the social media bullies who terrorized her while she was still alive. It appears we've put that all behind us. If you want to know if it's a crime to tell someone over social media to kill themselves if they are in clear danger of doing so, the short answer would appear to be that it isn't.

None of the dozens of schoolmates who found it funny to tag pictures of bleach with Amanda's name or found it necessary to exhort her to kill herself and then throw a party after she did have come forward, much less apologized. I've been told that several of them have actually since claimed online to have been Todd's friends.

As the years go by, memories fade, guilt ebbs and the people who did their best to make Amanda miserable will go on to live lives that fall within the bounds of normal — a life she was deprived of. They'll wear pink ribbons and light candles and tell other people how wrong bullying is.

And, until Coban was arrested, we heard very little in the way of investigating anyone other than Kody Maxson for extorting her. Keep in mind that Coban was investigated for other crimes, and it was only after his arrest for them that any connection to Amanda was found.

Kody himself has been quiet on social media since. A Twitter account named Kody Maxson is dedicated to Amanda's memory, but an account called Kody1206 (identified as belonging to a Kody M) is the one that many believe to be Maxson's own. Its posts are usually about the Vancouver area's public transit schedules.

In one post, he berates someone for posting a tweet about a late-arrving bus by writing: "shut your mouth about translink I'd love to see you do 8hrs of driving without being pissy, so stop complaining stupid whore."

He also thanks singing star Rihanna for posing for a nude photograph in a magazine and shows dismay that he's being followed by an account called PeytonLovesYouu (which features a photo of Peyton, the girl associated with him by the Daily Capper and others) with sad-face emoticon.

The account's holder largely ignores the many tweets that accuse him of complicity in the Todd case, but will occasionally lash out and then delete the response.

The few posts on the account that pre-date Amanda's death that remain are mostly invitations to video-chat on a site called TinyChat.

The Kody M account follows just 11 mostly corporate accounts, but it is followed by 143 people, many of them teenage girls.

No matter who runs that account, the real Dakota William Shain Maxson has been in serious trouble with the law since Amanda's death. Since then, he has faced charges for breaking and entering, leaving the province while on probation and theft of less than $5,000 value.

Quach and whoever Rora-anon is both appear to have fallen off the planet. It is just as likely, however, they are just using better aliases.

Cappers in general have been largely out of the news, but still appear to exist. On pua-zone.com — a site that promises users that they can "learn to pickup women and get laid for free" — a 24-year-old user who calls himself Cobra Kai in 2014 posted a how-to guide for getting girls to take their clothes off in video chats. At least he prefaces it with: "I'm gonna talk about capping and stuff that is in bad-taste and may be sort of illegal."

Many of the sites that hosted such chats have gone under, as have many of the sites — like anonib.com — on which "heroes" posted "win." Many other user-generated porn sites have stepped up their moderation of potentially illegal material, I've been told, and many of their users are more likely to report questionable images because they are not interested in being associated with cappers.

In all likelihood, cappers have once again moved a technological step or two ahead of those who would stop them. Without public attention and outrage to press law enforcement, they operate with little fear of being caught. It's hard to believe the concept of capping even would have made the news in the Amanda Todd case if there hadn't been a squabble among them that played out through The Daily Capper and Anonymous.

Naturally, Coban's trial will bring focus back onto them, at least briefly, and a few might even get caught, but they will probably just keep doing what they do and hope that they can hide their identities well enough to get away with it.

***

The aftermath of Todd's suicide raised a mirror to our society, and not a lot of what we saw was pretty. While lots of people rushed to offer sympathy, almost as many delighted in mocking the memory of the poor girl. And while it became fashionable to show support for Todd and girls like her, very little of concrete value came of it.

And the whole sad story also showed that law enforcement would sometimes prefer to leave serious crimes, like assault, to be sorted out by the aggressor and victim — especially if those involved were children. When it came to serious crimes like extortion, child pornography and sexual interference with a minor, all the local police in this case did was tell the victim to stay off the internet for a while. At least while she was still alive. Once she was dead, they got on the case and came up with very little.

But — thanks to Facebook's in-house security measures and international police forces — an arrest was eventually made in the case.

If the evidence in Coban's trial gets anywhere near the amount of publicity that the anti-bullying efforts did, there's a chance that more cappers will be exposed and even convicted. If a concerted effort is made, their community could be disrupted and actually made to realize that they were likely to face exposure and even punishment for distributing child pornography and extortion.

While tracking down and exposing the internet predators who target our young people might not be as easy as wearing a ribbon or commenting on a Facebook page, it might do us all more good.

Acknowledgements

Writing a book like this is always hard, but is much harder when few people will speak and even fewer will go on the record.

So, of course, I'd like to thank those few who did speak with me, especially Michael. Without him, the character of Amanda Todd would not have been as three-dimensional to me. Thanks for letting me know what it was like to know her.

I'd also like to thank the reporters who did their best to get to the bottom of this complex and frequently sordid story. Of particular note are those who worked in online media who seemed to be far more interested in the finding truth and less about furthering an agenda than those in the mainstream media were.

And I must thank the people at the Meager Press, who made the book possible.

Of course, I'm not under the delusion that the whole story has been told. If anyone reading this has more information pertaining to Amanda Todd, her bullies or her extortion, please let me know at themeagerpress@gmail.com so that we might be able to have a more detailed second edition.

www.ingramcontent.com/pod-product-compliance
Lightning Source LLC
LaVergne TN
LVHW051417080426
835508LV00022B/3124